The Strategic Intelligence of Trust
Life, an Evolutionary Force of Nature
By Roy Niles

Explanatory preface:

The book is concerned with the functional aspects of trust, distrust, and deception in all biological forms of life.

For 50 years or so, I've been concerned with the role played by trust in both the world and, as it would also appear, the universe. Trust seemed to me to be the glue that holds all of our interpersonal transactions together. Early on I'd tried to explain my feelings in this respect to my relatively well educated peers. No-one took my concerns with this concept seriously.

Subsequently I spent 40 years as a professional investigator, where an understanding of what to trust and what not was essential. As well as understanding the varieties of deceptive strategies that were used by the more psychopathic among us to mimic trust and trustworthiness. And like most of us, I believed that these were mainly human tactics, not necessarily those of the allegedly less intelligent life forms. Until, that is, I was made aware of the tactics of cephalopods, who seemed to mix deceptive tactics with trust in the non-deceptiveness of their targets in equal measure.

More informal study of the biological aspects of trust and deception followed. As well as a study of instinctive behaviors, and how they would have evolved to refine these tactics.
And then a study of evolutionary change in behaviors in general, a study of the predictive natures of our brains, and of our probabilistic and anticipatory forms of logical analysis,

The theory that eventually emerged was originally presented on the first few pages of this book, and apparently so poorly that few if any readers knew what I was talking about. I'd always believed that people learned more from drawing inferences than by rote instruction, but the inferences offered here were essentially as clear as mud.

What I was hoping to propose and demonstrate is this: Trust seems in fact the glue that holds all biological transactions together, but such glue would not be needed if there were not also mechanisms of deception in nature that required trust as a counter mechanism. Trust in other words not simply as a behavioral concept but a behavioral strategy. And while I'd said things to that effect in the original version of this book, they were expressed more as my conclusions rather than as an explanation for proposing the trust/deception thesis at the start.

I did write this however early on:
"Life: A self-sustaining chemical reaction (or energy system) with built in expectations.
Consciously or unconsciously it expects to be trusted if it does the one thing and deceived if it does the other.
And to find trust if it does the one thing and deceit if it does the other.
And to succeed by offering trust on the one hand or deceit on the other.
And all its calculating mechanisms are devised to predict consequences based on the probabilities associated with each of these expectations under all observable circumstances."

What I again failed to do, however, was present that as an hypothesis that I intended to offer evidence for, rather than as an already settled premise, no evidence needed, etc.
So even though the rest of the book remains as a somewhat stream of consciousness attempt at presenting various arguments in support of that hypothesis, it should have been made clear at the outset that making such an argument was my purpose. And made even clearer that the presentation of a litany of consequences that must, without argument, somehow have resulted from my premises, was not my purpose.

Further, I've failed to make it clear at the start that trust and deception are strategies that require intelligence to function, and further, as companion functions, strategies that must evolve in a heritable fashion. And I should have done a better job of explaining why we will need to have evolved them with the benefits of all our past experiences, as otherwise my various hypotheses will not apply at all to our evolving lives.

Unfortunately, most of what I did to that extent originally was state that: "All evolution is the proximate result of the entity involved reacting strategically to its experience." And although that was not meant as an hypothesis to be "proved" in this book, it should nevertheless have been offered as provisional to the acceptance of my evidence for the main hypothesis. Which is again, that trust and deception are complementary functions of all biological life, without which neither function would have existed, from the start, to evolve. And neither, as I hope to demonstrate, would have life.

The book has also been concerned with presenting a case for adaptive mutation, otherwise referred to as self engineering, and I may not have made it clear that under other and older versions of "natural selection" the proposal of any of my hypotheses here would be largely useless. And while I haven't attempted to offer much of my own evidence in support of these more intelligible evolutionary concepts, I have made repeated references to other authoritative sources that have made the case for intelligent self engineering of biological change very much to my personal satisfaction.

And, yes, I did speculate a bit as to the probability that the universe was operated as a complex of evolved and evolving strategic systems, from whence life's early choice making strategies would need to have evolved. Supporting references were made to the physicist John Wheeler, although I might have done well with some additional reference to the process philosophy of Whitehead,

And you'll find other speculation here involving the evolution of cooperation versus competition, the necessity of cultures for the communicative elements of learned experience, the development of empathy for cooperative purposes, the evolution of altruistic strategies, the group selection controversies and mistakes, etc. A lot of stuff for less than 100 or so pages. On the other hand, less than 100 pages was my goal, and if you need me to give a good reason for that, I don't know that I have one.

To return to where my efforts had originally begun, this is what I wrote in 2008 to start work on this book:

"Life: A self-sustaining chemical reaction (or energy system) with expectations.

In any developing organism, there must come an initial movement or probe, then a sensed response, and from that an "expectation" formed. Which - if and when later confirmed by another probe - would be equivalent to the formation of trust - except that so far there is no equivalent of distrust.

There is likely nothing yet that senses pain either, but at some point, the organism adapts to avoid destructive responses to its probes - such as destruction of the probing mechanism itself.

And from this non-confirmation of expectations rises a mechanism equivalent to suspicion of appearances - and thus the birth of distrust. And so at this point the organism is operating on a rudimentary trust or distrust basis.

While at this same time organisms competing for resources are adapting to take advantage of the weakness inherent in the methods used to fulfill expectations - by utilizing mechanisms that operate both offensively and defensively with tactics that are equivalent to what we now label as deception. These would include forms of mimicry and masking, for example.

And in organisms adapting in turn to these mechanical tactics, suspicion of appearances (or distrust) also becomes the mechanism equivalent to suspicion of deception. Even though it will be ages before any of these organisms has the ability or need to see or deal with either deception or trust as an abstract concept.
So to leap forward a bit here, we might now define and more broadly describe all life as we know it as follows:
Life: A self-sustaining chemical reaction (or energy system) with built in expectations.

Consciously or unconsciously it expects to be trusted if it does the one thing and deceived if it does the other.
And to find trust if it does the one thing and deceit if it does the other.
And to succeed by offering trust on the one hand or deceit on the other.

And all its calculating mechanisms are devised to predict consequences based on the probabilities associated with each of these expectations under all observable circumstances.

And whatever strategy each species then forms - and each individual in that species forms - will have been the result of combining these basic expectations with their experiences in a particular environment. And the genetic makeup of each species and individuals therein will have evolved and continue to evolve depending on which combinations of these basic strategies were used and how they contributed to their survival within the framework of each particular environment. And the number and variety of these combinations are virtually unlimited."

When I wrote that, I assumed that from the beginning all life forms were minimally intelligent. (Where they got intelligence without having it already is another story.) And that they used the trial and error process to accomplish whatever they had acquired as their purposes. And after several years of my own version of extensive research, I still think trial and error is not only how all of us on earth attempt to think, but quite possibly how all systems in the universe are likely to operate. (That other story?)

However, on the latter notion, I'm taking the word of some bona fide and certifiable scientists who are much smarter than myself in matters of the universe, and on the former, as regards our purposes, I'm taking my own word as being more philosophically curious than most about "why" things happen - as opposed, or in addition, to the more scientific goals of learning "how."

One thing I didn't mention in that early essay was why we've needed to compete for resources to begin with. Why wouldn't there have been enough to go around early on? I have no easy answer to that question, but when we talk later about how we're driven to cooperate in order to compete, I'll try to answer that. But first we need (I think) to understand how the central trust, distrust, and deception strategies of our lives must have evolved.

And as I noted earlier, by profession I've been an investigator, and after those 40 years of working first for the Federal Government and then in private practice, I do make claim to be more of a practical authority than most on the mechanisms of trust and deception. It helped that I'd managed (with the GI bill) to squeak out a B.A. at UC Berkeley in 1949, majoring in Philosophy, Psychology and English. And I'd long wanted to do some serious writing on the these subjects, but hadn't quite hit upon the hypothesis that blended these apparently opposing concepts into one.

In the meantime, I wrote a few private essays on this and that, and a slew of notes on the related subject of biological evolution - which at the time I was somewhat of an amateur about. And still am, except over the last few years I've taught myself what I think is now worth writing about in concert with the subject of the evolution of trust.

And so also in 2008 I wrote this:
"My best guess is that organisms "ask" abstract questions by looking for a pattern that fits within a series of possible to probable answers - if the expected or desired answers don't come, or are not reassuring, the organism feels fear, anxiety, boredom, etc.

These "question-answers" are built in through evolution, and not arrived at consciously, but can be augmented by using experience to better analyze the responses.

The range of anticipated answers would have to be set to correspond to a reliability scale, such as one with "fully reliable" at one end, and "fully unreliable" at the other. In between would be: maybe reliable, maybe not reliable, can't decide without more probes if reliable, etc.

The full range of these answers would vary from organism to organism, depending on its environment, phases of development, traditional predators, available prey, natural defenses, etc.

The degree of reliability is in inverse proportion to the degree of possible deception involved. Organisms need to assess the possibilities of deception, rather than its certainty. To confirm certainty before declining to act would simply put them at greater risk, and only the less vulnerable could afford to take the larger risks involved in this confirmation process. To paraphrase an old adage, sharks rush in where angelfish fear to tread."

I could change and update a lot of that, and improve the syntax, but this book is also about the nature of honesty, so I won't. As the old saying goes, If honesty is what you want, trust an honest man to at least be honest.

And in any case, honesty and deception are not necessarily antithetical - which I've tried to explain in another essay that I wrote to help out a former client - not expecting at the time to write a book about it. (So look for this essay at the end of this book.)

In the meantime, I wrote the following for one of my wife's old friends to read:

"Initial concept that is the basis of my work in progress: Brains, lizard or modern, are predictors of consequences. That was the cause for their development, the reason for that development, and the only way any decision making or action-reaction determinative process of any species, flora or fauna, could have developed. Any system that would have been fashioned to make decisions or prompt actions/reactions other than by the attempted prediction of probable consequences would not have been able to survive, let alone evolve.

Given a world in which we can observe that life essentially feeds on other life while at the same time trying to avoid being fed upon, in a seemingly endless circle of birth, death, and rebirth, this would appear as both an "a priori" and "a posteriori" deduction.

These predictions are necessarily based on a trial and error assessment of the degrees of success or failure involved in taking each of the perceivable and/or available options in each immediate or impending situation. Actions and reactions at this level are always based on the probability, rather than certainty, of future success, dependent in turn on the frequency of prior acts of a similar nature having attained the expected or hoped for degree of success under similar circumstances.

The calculations of course attempt to factor in the degrees of this similarity, and the development of our brains seems directly related to the survival value of any increase in the ability to assess all related factors observed or learned through previous experience - the ability to develop abstractions, if you will.
It's the uncertainty involved at the beginning and end of each calculation, whether made consciously, unconsciously, or by instinct, that makes the next step essentially one of trust that the outcome will be favorable, because certainty, regardless of what the modern brain may label as certain, was never a real part of this assessment process, and based on the resultant structure of our brains, can never be anything but an ultimately erroneous factor in that process.

Then I will go on to develop the theory that "trust predictability" is the basic mechanism underlying all human nature and the way every aspect of that nature has developed. It's essential to the process by which we go about satisfying needs, attaining pleasure or reward, avoiding pain or punishment, etc., etc., etc. One reason this seemingly hasn't been proposed before as the bottom line, is that most researchers seem to have have decided that the pleasure-pain principle, or reward-punishment principle, were the basic mechanisms involved, but in my way of thinking, the trust assessment mechanism underlies and accounts for the way these and all associated factors operate and play out. And it differs from what some regard as a mere true or false assessment.

I then talk about trust and it's flip side, deception, and my previous essays on the subject are a peek into the way I Intend to go about demonstrating my thesis."

At about this time, you can see how I'd decided to get this book written without further delay, using this rather unorthodox note posting fashion, since as of this writing (June, 2012) I was 85 years old and conventional means seemed no longer a sensible option. I've selected some of the better pieces of my last few years of notes to tell, as it were, my story. (At least for this first intended volume, as my notes alone cover several hundred pages.)

And I'll do my best to edit the whole shebang from time to time, but if I die in the process, at least there should be something of substance left to publish - for whatever it's hopefully worth.

But let's move on to these thoughts written also in 2008. They involve the choice making mechanism, which in my view effectively separates the living from the non-living, and has enabled us to trust from the outset:

"Notes on Trust-Deception Dichotomy Label
Regarding all actions involving element of trust: Consider if instinct ever causes action that requires no choice - is there any such example? It would seem so only when the choice was made by the circumstance, not the animal. But if the circumstance was one instinctively recognized as trustworthy in the sense that this recognition was the signal to act, then the choice was still the animal's.

Similarly if it recognized a signal that the situation was dangerous, and the instinct was then to react against the danger, the type of reaction was again chosen by the instinctive process.

Thus the circumstance didn't choose, even if it may itself have been the result of some other choice. In any case, the signal sent out triggered a form of choice by the animal, as different circumstances triggered different responses, no matter how automatic and uniform.

So is the dichotomy one of safety-danger, rather than trust-deception? Or both? No and no. Safety to danger is the range of the trust scale. Deception involves danger, and if discovered is a signal of impending danger. But the "process" of deception involves the masking of danger to encourage trust and therefor breach the opponent's defenses against danger; and the process also includes the masking of the potential victim to appear other than an inviting target.

So more thinking is in order about the so-called "dichotomy," but isn't the difference that trust and deception are both functions, while safety and danger are concepts or descriptions of attributes? So trust-deception is the functional dichotomy that is involved in decisions that ascertain degrees of safety or danger. No?

Larger meaning of deception as used in this context: People may have missed the importance of its function here because they tend to put a moral dimension on the mechanism of deception, where in nature there are no such moral dimensions.

Morality is a human concept, and our primitive brains developed without reference to such arbitrary boundaries between appropriate and inappropriate social interactions.

(We do make instinctive decisions as to right and wrong, but based mainly on the assessment of more immediate consequences, and on a scale of safety versus danger, plus a sometimes conflicting scale of pleasure versus pain. And the ultimate arbiter of these conflicts is, in effect, the trust versus deception scale.)

As an illustration of this misunderstanding of its overall function, a prominent contemporary philosopher has argued that while all deception involves secrecy, all secrecy does not involve deception. This is said to be so because not all secrecy is meant to deceive. Examples are given showing how some secrecy is meant to protect privacy or intimacy, etc. But these are not really examples of a lack of deception - they are examples of deception used to conceal a possible area of weakness rather than to conceal potential danger. And in fact, these examples add support to the concept of a trust-deception dichotomy.
Deception in all these cases is meant to make the deceiving animal appear trustworthy, whether it is because it might on the one hand appear too dangerous to be trusted, or on the other, too weak to be trusted.

And again the application of these functions differs as the situations that confront the animals are seen to differ. And one of the functions of deception, of course, is to deceive others as to the nature of the situation as well as to the nature of the deceiving animal's ability to take advantage of that situation.

In human society, which is essentially where the understanding of these concepts would and could make a difference, we unconsciously assess degrees of trustworthiness by both the nature of any deception perceived and the circumstances under which we might have perceived it. These circumstances include the cultural context involved as well as all other perceivable variables.

Secrets uncovered are often seen as excusable deception, and therefor not a reason to withhold trust - such as when the motives involved appear not only to be for the protection of the deceiving party, but also for the person or persons being protected from harm by that particular deception. (Refer to a discussion of white lies for examples.)"

Now I don't know that I was right when I spoke of morality as only a human concept, or when referring to "our" primitive brains without designating some of these as ancestral, and some of these ancestors in turn as animals. But ideas evolve in our minds and cultures, and much of the above have since evolved in my mind as well (if not all that much in my culture).

And I then added this to the above essay:

"What is the difference, if any, between a "friend or foe" assessment and one intrinsic to the trust-deception dichotomy? "Friend or foe" is not an independent strategy - it's part of the trust-deception function, which is also the strategic mechanism for deciding if and when the organism itself should act as a friend or foe, as well as how to determine and react to the presence of a friend or a foe.

"Can it be trusted or is it deceptive?" This would appear to be the basic consideration, and an integral part of asking: "Is safe or is it dangerous?" Decisions about the presence of danger, to be the most effective, would seem to require answers to questions that invariably involve the possibility of deception.

For example, where sensory signals show no patterns recognized as dangerous, a question would have to be "Are these signals also consistent with possible deception?" The organism has to ask itself that question before taking further action, and that action will usually involve some sort of probe to test the accuracy of it's initial impressions.

Organisms that develop the best testing methods, and in effect the best follow-up questions, will have the best chances of long-term survival. Those that don't probe or test will certainly fall prey to to the deceptive strategies of predators, and there is no question that those strategies have existed long enough to have made such testing an evolutionary requirement.

Where sensory systems have recognized patterns as dangerous, either from inherited instincts or "trial and error" experience, the basic questions would still need to be, "How dangerous is this object or situation?" "Is there deception involved that would conceal even more danger - such as mimicry of a clumsy foe to conceal a more lethal one?" Or, "Is there less danger involved, and the appearance intended to conceal weakness, mimicking strength and fending off predators accordingly?"

Further, a trust-deception assessment is applicable to every action an organism takes or is able to contemplate, and not just those involving safety and danger. The judgement of any quality of another organism or circumstance where need or desire plays a role depends on the same sort of assessment to determine the extent of desirableness and to predict success or failure, or any combinations thereof.

It isn't likely that this methodology would not be used in one set of circumstances when it is readily available for application to all other types of situations where the prediction of consequences is essential to success. And it is simply not conceivable that a "friend or foe" assessment would survive as a modus operandi without a need to assess the possibility of deception being inherent to the equation.

I've speculated since that the feeling of danger is not only equivalent to suspicion of deception, it's much more the same thing than I'd first thought. It appears to me now that the suspicion of deception had in a way become the sense of danger - and suspicion separated itself from that sense at the same time, and tactically evolved to predict deception. And deception has evolved in turn as a strategy for avoidance of predictability!

And so I also wrote the following, published in part on a blog I write for, which concerns how ideas of truth or falsity have evolved to suit our modern brains:

"Assumptive Differences - Reliability versus True or False
The noted logician, Bertrand Russell, at age 92, was reported to have asserted that reason had its limitations: "Beware of rational argument," he said; "you need only one false premise in order to prove anything you please by logic." Leading me to another illustration of how, when it comes to survival strategies, the rational parts of our brain are more prone to error than we might have suspected:

Take for example this version of the liar paradox (also a subject of Russell's writings), which was ascribed to the ancient Greek, Epimenides the Cretan, who said that, 'All Cretans are liars.' We have here a statement that seemingly cannot, by traditional logic, be judged either true or false.

But instead of just reading that statement, imagine that you actually met Epimenides, and he said to you personally: "All Cretans are liars." Your first reaction might be to wonder why, being a Cretan, would he say that, even if he thought it was true? And secondly, does he mean all Cretans always lie, or that no Cretan always tells the truth, or no Cretan ever tells the truth?

Your "emotional" or "limbic" brain is thus examining signals reflecting the degree of probability that the statement is or is not reliable, as reliability is the key concept here. In a face to face encounter, this brain will automatically consider the speaker's motives, rather than operate from a presumption that the statement will be either true or false. It's the "rational" brain's assumption that things have to be one or the other that creates the apparent paradox.

"Paradox" has been defined as an assertion that is essentially self-contradictory, though based on a valid deduction from acceptable

premises. And of course there's no paradox if Epimenides is simply lying himself. Or if he is simply wrong and doesn't see the contradiction implicit in his also being a Cretan.

But because we can't make a valid deduction without having more evidence available, we will intuitively treat the statement as unreliable, yet not necessarily know why, or know how to resolve the apparent contradictions.

Clearly, the assumptive premise that a thing is either true or false is the essential flaw in this process, and without the input from the emotional brain that the statement may be deliberately deceptive, the rational brain, given the initial premise, has a harder time reaching a conclusion that this aspect of "reliability" is in fact the answer.

The inference to be drawn here is that a "true or false" assessment alone is not sufficient as part of a successful survival strategy. If, for example, organisms were built to assume true first and false later, they would fall prey to any organisms that assumed false first and true later.

And the latter group would then fall prey to any that made no such assumptions without an instinctive assessment of the evidence for any combination of these attributes, and the implications of that combination. It's these limbic system strategies, selected by the evolutionary process, that in the long term have contributed the most to our survival.

And these strategies recognize that other organisms, whether predators, competitors, or even cooperative entities, don't use false signals for any purpose except to be deceptive. "Trueness" and "falseness" apply to the means used to attain ends, rather than to the ends themselves.

These ends, or goals, are the satisfaction of needs and desires, and the strategies to attain them necessarily involve assessments of the degree of deception discernible, and of the trust that can be placed in the signals that at the same time appear lacking in deception.

Reliability, which is essentially a form of trustworthiness, is being sought through these strategies, and the concepts of "true" and "reliable" are not interchangeable. Truth is a part of the reliability assessment, but the

degree of predictability encompassed is its fundamental component. Brains are essentially predictors of consequences, and, if my theories are correct, "trust predictability" represents the basic methodology involved.
This illustration was meant to demonstrate some of the difficulties we have in implementing this process, as well as in understanding it. "

Well then, is everything that can't be trusted deceptive? Perhaps not, as if it's not alive, then at least it's not intentionally deceptive. Although, if it were built by life, it could well have been intended by the builder to deceive us. Are geological formations that contain and protect microbial life deceptive? No, but the life forms that they were intended, by life's efforts, to protect, have contributed to their building in some fashion to fool potential foes.

Begging the question of course as to what's 'truly' alive, what isn't, and what's somehow in between. We can't trust that we know that, or ever will. So must we distrust the overhanging rock as it can potentially fall upon us? Well yes, except that you are in fact distrusting your own ability to predict when it will or will not fall, be caused or not be caused, by the forces that are there behind all accidents, to come loose. Forces that may or may not serve other beings with deceptive purposes.

And where it would seem that deception is at least a logical process, it would also seem to some philosophers that the universe itself is attempting to be logical, and therefor, since it's never still but always active, attempting to act logically as well.

The implication being that if not acting logically for a purpose - which would be at present to control its essentially chaotic nature - without logic, it would become uncontrollably chaotic. Meaning I presume that the universe would effectively freeze up. But now it appears that I've digressed, so if I can, I'll come back to these disputable presumptions later.

Ok. let's open up another area of consideration here. Such as why do I see our microbial and other ancestors as having developed any such strategies from experience, when many of the most popular evolutionary biologists see their and our evolution as essentially the inevitable result of accidents, and hold that evolution in general neither had nor served our special purposes to start with?

First of all, do single celled organisms really think? This source, taken from my notes, among many others to be found online, suggests they do:

Cell Mol Life Sci. 2007 Jul;64(14):1801-4.
Do cells think? Ramanathan S, Broach JR.

Source, Bell Laboratories, Alcatel-Lucent Technologies, Murray Hill, New Jersey 07974, USA.

Abstract
A microorganism has to adapt to changing environmental conditions in order to survive. Cells could follow one of two basic strategies to address such environmental fluctuations. On the one hand, cells could anticipate a fluctuating environment by spontaneously generating a phenotypically diverse population of cells, with each subpopulation exhibiting different capacities to flourish in the different conditions.
Alternatively, cells could sense changes in the surrounding conditions - such as temperature, nutritional availability or the presence of other individuals - and modify their behavior to provide an appropriate response to that information. As we describe, examples of both strategies abound among different microorganisms.
Moreover, successful application of either strategy requires a level of memory and information processing that has not been normally associated with single cells, suggesting that such organisms do in fact have the capacity to 'think'.

And if you need more convincing on this subject, please read such books as Wetware: A Computer in Every Living Cell, Dennis Bray.
And better yet, read about smart bacteria in papers such as this from James A. Shapiro, Department of Biochemistry and Molecular Biology, University of Chicago:
Bacteria are small but not stupid: Cognition, natural genetic engineering, and sociobacteriology.
http://shapiro.bsd.uchicago.edu/2006.ExeterMeeting.pdf

And then I more recently wrote this comment on a blog, Evolution for Everyone, then run by the evolutionary biologist, David Sloan Wilson:

"*OK, I'll summarize some of what is being discovered as succinctly as I can without making it an argument:*
The cells that retain the memory of an experience then pass on that memory to those they have been divided into. Inheritance of acquired memories of experience, no? And many generations appear to be affected - and the effects of this experience can't be completely erased from the genome if the experience itself is replicated or repeated in a particular environment. And this seems one of the ways that cells evolve to anticipate and deal strategically with a multitude of problems.

Because it seems to be the present case with most social species that their form of culture is a preserver of learned strategies, some of which by reason of their effectiveness will become instinctive, and our earliest life forms may have started that instinctive process by passing the memories of learning directly through cell division.

While later on when sexual selection and the like evolved, the mechanism for passing on what would be needed as socially instructive was a "culture" that required its lessons taught at least by example - and thus evolved our methods of communication for sharing memories that was more efficient then cell memory copying, especially as that original method of procreation did not apply all that well to multi cellular organisms.

Which leads one, or at least me, to opine that all evolution from the getgo was and had to have been a social/cultural phenomenon. Learning creates strategies which create forms to fit, which gain experience that strategies adapt to, and through cultural sharing by example or advances in communication, spread the impetus for re-adaptation throughout the groups accordingly.

Cultures assist in the heritability of acquired characteristics: Cultures provide the platform for their strategic development and purpose, and in addition help "spread the word" that accelerates the acquisition of these strategies "instinctively." Strategy is the function of intelligence. The form

alone has no intelligence. It can't choose, even though it's a cause of choice. The function chooses form and/or chooses how it will be caused to adapt.
There's more of course, but cutting to the chase, I don't think there is a non-adaptive side of the evolutionary coin and that indeed it's more than possible that "all traits in the end evolve from strategically successful behaviors."

Dr. Wilson replied that, "This is cool stuff." (Did he wholeheartedly agree? Not really.)

So here's a relevant excerpt from the James Shapiro paper referenced just above (and hopefully it will induce you to read the paper):
"The realization that most DNA changes in bacteria (and eukaryotes, too) occur by the action of natural genetic engineering systems removes the source of variation in the genome from the category of stochastic events or unpredictable accidents and places it in the context of cellular biochemistry. This reclassification has major conceptual consequences because cellular biochemistry is subject to regulation and operates in predictable ways."

And in addition, you might want to read this paper:
Social Learning and the Baldwin Effect, by David Papineau
http://www.kcl.ac.uk/ip/davidpapineau/Staff/Papineau/OnlinePapers/SocLearnBald.htm

Papineau, Professor of Philosophy of Science in the Department of Philosophy at King's College London, wrote:
"Let me conclude with an empirical prediction. If my doubly Baldwinian social learning mechanism has indeed been important for the evolution of complex behaviours, as I have hypothesized, then we should expect to find, somewhat paradoxically, that complex innate behaviours are more common in species that are good social learners than in other species. True, any such correlation will be diluted by the fact that the relative costs of learning and genetic control will not always favour bringing socially learned traits under genetic control (in the way I have been assuming since section 2.1). Even so, if I am right in thinking that social learning vastly expands the range of behaviours open to genetic assimilation, species that are good general social learners should still display significantly more

complex innate behaviour than other species. Unfortunately I lack the expertise to assess this prediction myself. But I would be very interested indeed to know whether or not the comparative zoological data bear it out."

I could go on with the various references, but this was meant to be a short first volume of my (potential) books. However, you may want to take a look at things like this in future:

The Calculative Nature of Microbe–Mineral Interactions
Authors: Caldwell, D. E.1; Caldwell, S. J.2
Source: Microbial Ecology, Volume 47, Number 3, April 2004 , pp. 252-265 (14)
Publisher: Springer

Abstract:
"Microorganisms continually redefine themselves at many levels, including the molecule, cell, and community. Although it was initially assumed that this resulted from the genesis of information within DNA alone, it has since been shown that innovation originates at multiple levels.
This occurs through calculative units, each unit consisting of two proliferating structures, one nested within the other and each undergoing changes in structural geometry that affect the proliferation rate of the other. For example, the recombination of genetic structures affects the proliferation of community structures, and the recombination of community structures affects the proliferation of genetic structures. The proliferation of a nested series of structures (e.g., genes proliferating within cells, cells proliferating within communities, communities proliferating within ecosystems) results in a logic circuit that calculates the form and function of each structural element in the series. In this situation each element functions as both a habitat and an inhabitant (environment and organism), and it is this dichotomy that determines the balance of nature. Nested geological structures, such as minerals and continents, also proliferate and redefine themselves in much the same way. Microbe–mineral interactions thus link nested biological calculations to an analogous set of nested geological calculations. Examples include the microorganisms involved in the nucleation (proliferation) of ferric hydroxides, carbonates, silicates, and ice crystals."

A lot more complicated than a blind watchmaker at work, I'd say. Certainly there seem to be some real purposes a work there. Although now would be a good time to agree on how we define the concept of purpose:

purpose l'pərpəsl
noun
the reason for which something is done or created or for which something exists : the purpose of the meeting is to appoint a trustee l the building is no longer needed for its original purpose.
• a person's sense of resolve or determination : there was a new sense of purpose in her step as she set off.
• (usu. purposes) a particular requirement or consideration, typically one that is temporary or restricted in scope or extent : pensions are considered as earned income for tax purposes.
verb [trans.] formal
have as one's intention or objective

purposive l'pərpəsiv; pər'pō-l
adjective
having, serving, or done with a purpose : teaching is a purposive activity.

But then see this abstract re how this should apply to what must actually be our purposive forms:

Thinking about Life
The History and Philosophy of Biology and Other Sciences
10.1007/978-1-4020-8866-7_15
Paul S. Agutter and Denys N. Wheatley

"Living organisms act purposefully, and their individual parts — organs, cells, organelles, molecules — fulfill purposes for the whole. Those purposes 'come from within'; animals, for example, seek food and mates for themselves. In contrast, the purposes of technological products such as drawing pins, hat-stands and washing machines 'come from outside'; they are defined by their makers and users. A washing machine does not wash clothes for itself.

Ever since the Scientific Revolution it has been agreed that the inanimate world of rocks, rivers, stars, clouds etc. does not act purposefully. It is to be understood in mechanistic not teleological terms.
An inanimate object is not for anything or anyone; whatever it does is a consequence of antecedent causes. That implies a basic difference between biology on the one hand and physics and chemistry on the other. If biology is to be wholly compatible with physics, that difference needs to be resolved. We must be able to make complete mechanistic sense of purpose in biology."

So let's look into the subject of biological purposes a bit more here! And by the way, I don't necessarily agree with the above as to inanimate objects lacking any form of purpose. But I'll save that part of the argument for later.

For now, I'll boldly state the following: You can't understand logic without some understanding of inference, and can't understand inference without some understanding of intention, and can't understand intention without some understanding of purpose.

And I'll wager that you can't demonstrate that any part of that above statement is wrong. Simply because all intentional behaviors will appear to have at least one immediate and inferable purpose. (And as I'll also argue later, unintentional/accidental actions will be made to serve our purposes as well.)

And a better philosopher than I'll ever be wrote this:
In the pragmatic way of thinking in terms of conceivable practical implications, every thing has a purpose, and its purpose is the first thing that we should try to note about it.
Charles Sanders Peirce, the founder of American pragmatism.

But if there are in fact biological purposes, how would they in any case relate to what is still considered by many to be the essential purposeless of evolution? Well, it's my opinion and my argument that all evolution is the proximate result of the entity involved reacting strategically to its experience. So evolution doesn't have to "have" a purpose other than to "serve" the purposes of the entities that use evolutionary strategies to evolve. And what I'm attempting to do here is reveal what those strategies more reliably consist of.

So is it then the purpose of life to simply exercise its biological strategies? Yes, although of course it's neither the exercise nor the strategies that are the "simple" parts. But then why do strategies with purposes exist in our world or our universe to begin with? For now, my answer would have to be that the universe has always consisted of strategically evolving systems - an answer that for me is reasonable if only because all others I've come across are less so. I'll talk more about that later as well, but for now, the purposes that life acquired and acquires on its own are where I have the need - and needs fuel purposes - to focus on.

But biological strategies and their functional apparatus clearly have evolved for a purpose; they are algorithmic structures, they enable choice making by providing a range of optional responses to stimuli. These tactical responses are probative and anticipatory. They enable comparative analysis, testing expectations, assessing feedback, assigning relevant meaning to the data accordingly. They allow for storage of results and continued analysis of data from the feedback loop, adjusting the relevance of the stored results continuously. In short, they allow for learning. They form the trial and error structures of biological intelligence.

I remember once being asked whether an organism's purpose is to survive in order to evolve. In other words, surviving with evolving as its goal perhaps? But this is an example of the faulty questions we are faced with when it comes to providing what, if we accepted the premises as valid, could only result in faulty answers. The best way to answer such a question is to amend its premise, and consider it more likely that organisms evolve to survive. And that perhaps since all things are observed to be in a constant state of change, that such change itself must be in service of all "evolving" processes.

Evolution in some sense is not optional in our universe. If the universe, as I have argued elsewhere, is indeterminate, it will have to involve some changes caused by unintended accident, but all that tells us is that evolution is not an inherently accidental process, since even accidents, if we are required to use them to our advantages, have come to serve our own biologically intelligent purposes. (OK, that sounds a bit too complicated, but I can't think of a better way to put it right now without over simplifying it.)

So, we (on behalf of all living beings) are now considering that our purposes are to carry out what can be loosely called our cooperative yet ultimately individual survival strategies, and also help to evolve them as part of that overall process.

And what motivates our purposive attempts are our instinctive assessments of everything outside (and some inside) ourselves that must be dealt with according to the degree that we can assess their trust-worthiness. And thus make all choices partly on the basis of that provisional and always circumstantial series of ongoing assessments. While not being aware, unconsciously or otherwise, of the extent to which, in the process, we are doing most of this at all. Ouch.

Here's something from my notes that may have a bearing on what I've presented, at least as a tribute to my reasonableness:
"When you have a logically consistent explanation of why your theory is correct and how the predictions it enables have acted to confirm its accuracy and utility, then you will be convinced of your rationality in this endeavor. But rationality is to that extent a relative assessment, since logical consistency does not require a certainty as its outcome. And there's a certain inevitability to contend with that a different set of assumptions will eventually be needed to explain newly discovered inconsistencies between predictive consequences and actual events.

So as to that portended future, lets look at this from Wikipedia to deal with at least one of any number of potential objections, the accusation of some false claim of "teleonomy," in that I'm projecting evolution as an intentionally goal seeking process when it supposedly isn't.

"Teleonomy is the quality of apparent purposefulness and of goal-directedness of structures and functions in living organisms that derive from their evolutionary history, adaptation for reproductive success, or generally,

due to the operation of a program. Teleonomy is related to programmatic or computational aspects of purpose.
The term was coined to stand in contrast with teleology, which applies to ends that are planned by an agent which can internally model/imagine various alternative futures and, enables intention, purpose and foresight. A teleonomic process, such as evolution, produces complex products without the benefit of a guiding foresight."

And at this point it's I that must object to this definition. In my conception of the process, it's either teleonomic with at least a short term purpose, or we will now need either a newer definition or a newer word. Because while there is no guiding agent outside of our biological selves to model our futures, it has become clear to me (and to those I have previously cited) that we do and have done our own trial and error self engineering process modeling quite satisfactorily, thank you.

And I see that there was a bit of a concession in that article where the current status was that "*Teleonomy is closely related to concepts of emergence, complexity theory and self-organizing systems.*" Well, OK I guess.

Also I wrote this in my notes: "*And then, for one more thing, there's a fluidity of purpose and subpurposes involved that are continuously revising the goals dependent on constant feedback from the effects of prior purposive efforts. Hardly an "ultimate goal" directed process.*"

And I'm sure to hear from those that seem to dominate the scientific blogosphere who don't believe evolution is concerned with purpose at all. Talk Origins Archive, unfortunately, has a good example under "Bombardier Beetles and the Argument of Design."

"*It may seem obvious that the purpose of a bombardier beetle's defense mechanism is to protect it against predators--and indeed it is effective at such defense [Eisner, 1958]--but that is only our view; without reading the beetle's mind, we can't know what its purpose is. In fact, the bombardier mechanism is probably just a reflex, since it doesn't fire at some predators (such as some human collectors) and it does fire at some non-predators (such as a pair of forceps wielded by an experimenter). Ultimately, statements of purpose are statements of our own beliefs and nothing more."*

Now this is the common view of those who can't accept that organisms react strategically to their experience. The article above goes on to say that: *"The bombardier beetle's defense doesn't work because that's its purpose; we attribute that purpose because the beetle's defense works."*

I think they meant to say it doesn't work for that 'reason' since clearly they don't equate reasons to purposes when it comes to natural selection's singularly stochastic features. They're arguing that the defense works simply because it turned out to work. A mechanism that the beetle was surprised to find it had, perhaps, and apparently can't always get to work right. Was that blind watchmaker a rascal or what!

Some other comments I had earlier written about biological purposes follow:
"Deception for my purposes may need to be defined as either purposeful or serving of some purpose that expects to find it beneficial." OK, done.

"Some space-selective mirror neurons change their response when a barrier blocks access. As the article's authors suggest, mirror neurons may contribute to understanding "what others are doing" and these space-selective properties might help to decide "how I might interact with them". My comment was however that this mechanism is likely concerned that the blocked access conceals something from which to determine intent, capacity for harm, as well as capacity for reward, etc. So deception suspected as the purpose of concealment seems of particular concern to this function." OK, obvious. We'll talk about the general subject of this empathetic function later.

"Actually Lamarck was correct in hypothesizing that evolution was purposeful, but as a human, he was thinking of purpose as a long term proposition, while evolution "thinks" of purpose in extremely short term increments." OK, I guess, even though evolution doesn't really think for the organism.

"Regarding purpose: Even if all genetic changes were caused by accidental mutations, there would be no evolutionary adaptation until trial and error sorted out the potentially successful results.
No matter how you slice and dice it, the organism must react to its environment, even if with the simplest of strategies. It tries because it has to. That's its purpose.
Life forms are molecular structures that have acquired the capacity to seek out and compete for energy. That seeking out is their purpose. The competition determines their strategy. The relative effectiveness of their strategies is determinant of their evolution." (More or less OK for now).

"Which brings up the likelihood that there are a multitude of purposefully directed acts of deception at every moment somewhere in the cosmos, and that may result in misperceptions by observers other than those initially targeted and expected to be the deceived. So that there may be masked events that we might consider as hidden by simple circumstances, as well as by our own lack of the sensory apparatus to see around or behind some obstructions, but that were in fact masked to achieve some purpose which we were never, and could never have been, expected to discern."
So is that like the sound of the tree falling alone in the forest? Nah. The tree didn't likely fall on purpose, even though it served the strategic purposes of its programming - which was probably not to be the cause of accidents,

Well, this listing of my notes might go on forever if I didn't for the moment stop with this:
"Here is the official position of some evolutionary biologists, taken from a paper on enzyme evolution: "Evolution does not work towards any particular direction, nor is there a goal; the underlying processes occur spontaneously during reproduction and survival of the whole organism."
Perhaps what is not understood is that there can be purpose simply in a series of incremental and purposive (i.e., calculated) reactions, the initial purposive impetus being that to start or continue such a process has more often than not been beneficial to the organism.
The secret, if any, is to understand that all long term progress is the result of the cumulative effects of short term strategies.
Life adapts its strategies "intelligently" and alters its apparatus and structure accordingly."

OK, I buy most of that. 'Spontaneously' is a term that always troubles me, however.

But for the moment let's close this section with some comments I've made (my blog, etc., 2010) about proposing a possible Hierarchy of Purposes, just as there had been a Hierarchy of Needs presented years ago.

"I began to realize that in addition to there being what some have called a hierarchy of needs, which our cognitive systems have been "designed" to address, there must be a hierarchy of the purposes that go along with those needs. As in a way, our essential purpose as living beings is to satisfy the needs that the very existence of life requires. And the purposes may not be ranked in accordance with any particular need, but with a relative importance of each need.

And that will depend on the expectations of when it becomes necessary for our satisfaction and how. A hierarchy that won't be consistent with the presently constituted need-ranking hypothesis.
And needs after all create purposes. And those purposes in turn progressively refine and add to the needs that serve them.
Giving me something new to think about which hadn't been on the conscious agenda at all before today.

And since posting the above on my blog and elsewhere, I have noted that the "hierarchy of purpose" concept is not exactly new, as the psychologist William McDougall [1871 - 1938] viewed the mind as an hierarchically integrated system of purposes. I discovered this when I also thought "purposivism" might be a good word to coin, and found that term also used with respect to the 'purposive psychology' theories developed in large part by McDougall."

And with that, we move to this next section, about the evolution of all life's trustful and deceptive strategies. With their purposes still inescapably a central issue. (So for now I'll leave setting up an actual and credible hierarchy to someone else.)

Everything that exists has acquired the purpose of surviving the nature of continual change. That seems to me to be a given, and I'll try to back that up in greater detail later.

And so, put more concisely, all evolution has been at bottom the process of surviving change. If your physical dimensions don't need to be realigned to survive, and your instinctive behaviors don't need significant revision, your cultural learning systems will still be the necessary elements of your lives that continually evolve, and all else about your living systems will eventually/inevitably follow. (More on those cultural systems also later.)

And all of your strategies and tactics for survival, instinctive or otherwise, have been at some earlier point learned. As previously noted, all our earthly organisms will have acquired instincts that involve the necessity, unconsciously or more consciously, for some degree of trust in their surroundings, their companions, and in the end themselves.
And in that continually changing process, will have learned when best to turn that trust to some degree of distrust as well.
And will have developed all of their particular species' strategies, from the learned to the instinctive, and to the re-learned, accordingly.
And will all "know" that there's no such thing as perfect trust, but not necessarily ever know that there's some very perfect deception out there.

However, until humans and the like arose, there was likely no such concept as either trust or deception. We invented the words and thus seem to think we've invented, or at least perfected, the practices. But we haven't. Deception as the adversarial component of trust is a practice that may well have been a staple of all universal systems for all of time.
What we did, however, is attempt to control it, by trying to define and codify its culturally unacceptable aspects. Deterring unwanted acts in turn by punishment, more often based on the bare elements of the actions than on a closer examination of their intents and purposes.

Thus with us, deception as a tactic took on the aspect of dishonesty, where in the animal kingdom, the distinction as to what would or would not be trustworthy depended much more on purposes than actions. Honesty for its own sake has had no meaning in that world.

So called lower forms of life "see" their uses of mimicry, misdirection, concealment, and the like as vital to their overall well being and survival. They would offer no trust to others of their species that did not do their best to carry out their cooperatively executed crafty, sly and cunning strategies. (And of course, it turns out we do much the same, but we're not necessarily to be trusted for the doing of it.)

But back to the necessities of early organismic life, given that the main diet of these forms would arguably have soon become other life, all forms of life were and still are in some sense predatory, Whether they preferred meat or vegetable matter made a difference, but it should be noted that both flora and fauna have developed strategies to protect themselves from the excess of other's appetites. Fruit was made to be eaten, but not the tree, and not necessarily the leaves.

In the oceans for example, creatures replicate as if they expect a large part of their progeny to be eaten, and adapt their replicative strategies accordingly. Some conceal their progeny in various ways, while others overwhelm the potential predators with numbers. Camouflage and mimicry are perhaps the most common deceptive strategies, yet still not simple ones, because each side of the game can sense the others dangers.

Potential predators will thus act to counter the suspicions of their prey by masking signs of their immediate intentions and abilities to act on them. Even dedicated predators such as sharks will use body language to mask their purposes until they're in position to attack. In other words the game is always to outsmart the other side, and worse, there are no referees or rules to make it "fair." Fairness is more related to cooperation, and while predators and prey cooperate on some levels, its only for mutually beneficial purposes, and not for the sport of it. (Although some may play with you before they kill and eat you. Practice making perfect, I'd guess.)

When predator and prey outsmart each other, it's not, and it can't be, by any means except deception. We should perhaps take that as an example that when we humans feel we are outsmarting someone, it's again because we think, at least in our animalistic subconscious, that we've been successfully deceiving them.

And this tells us all life forms that have survived over time in this game are not just intelligent, but quite cleverly so. The behavioral traits that have evolved to enable them to both fashion and carry out these tactics can't have been selected by some incredibly lucky series of stochastic accidents. (Although if you're still inclined to think so, then you're free to do so.)

From my notes: *"Accident may have played a vital role in our early evolution but life takes advantage of accident and we rely too much on the continuing role of accident as an evolutionary mechanism when we fail to realize it's the type of cause that gives, and by it's very nature will not keep on giving."*

Here's a bit more sophisticated version from my notes regarding the evolutionary stages of suspicion and the nature and purpose of its development mechanistically:

"Certain sensations will trigger the need in an organism to calculate the odds or chances that a failure to confirm certain expectations is an indication of danger, and, depending on its capabilities, to calculate the odds of success for taking one or more available options in response.

In return, the predator - that this organism will have been forced to adapt its tactics to - is at the same time adapting its efforts at the concealment of its dangerousness - necessarily involving means of overcoming the effective probing and other sensory detectors of its prey. Through this process, predators interfere with the ability of prey to calculate evasive responses effectively. Thus the process of deception has both cooperatively and competitively developed.

The victim's calculations are thrown off by the altering of the sensual information that those calculations must depend on for accuracy. The predatory organism has used its mechanism for detecting signs of danger to function as a detector of deception from its intended prey as well. Each "learns" in the process, in whatever role it takes as prey or predator, to mimic the tactics of its particular adversaries." Cool.

I'll add a few more comments here about some common strategies, but then I'll move on. Other books have been written about the prevalence of such strategies if you want to learn more. This book is meant to demonstrate my hypothesis that such strategies have been necessary for the living of all of our lives. Those who will intuitively accept that may go on to help me prove this in the future. Those who don't, won't.

And let me note there are aggressively predatory animals that show little fear of potentially deceptive strategies that could overpower them. They are confidant of their ability to overcome any of the tactics they have learned from experience to expect. But in some ways this leaves them particularly vulnerable to changes that allow invasion of unknown species with unknown tactics into their environment. Self trust can go awry, as we'll talk about next. For now, note also that suspicion of deception could be triggered by lack of another's expected cooperation, leaving one to suspect an alternative approach simply by the process of elimination.

And, as you might ask, do our trusted choices always face the possibility of deception? In one way or another, they have to. Even choosing an inanimate object makes you think about its quality, any hidden defects possible, etc. One way or another, our suspicions are always with us. Our predictive capabilities won't work without them. (Self trust should not be absolute in other words.)

And I see on my notes that I once wrote "*culture consists of a set of mutually understood rules as to both covert and overt acts that are or are not seen as acceptable, and of rules by which the unacceptable are to be dealt with.*"
And I should have referenced the rules by which those acceptably deceptive actors, also known paradoxically as the self-trusted, are rewarded as well.

So, what is self trust anyway, and why is it not only important to us as humans, but was of crucial import to the successful strategies of life from the get-go? We might call it self confidence and self respect but those terms are mostly metaphors for what we need to recognize as the real thing - the element of trust that resides within and is essential to the organizing of what we've labeled as life's organismic systems. Self trusting systems might be a better label.

It's been written that self trust is uniquely human, but it's not that at all. There'd arguably be no life without that central element of strategy - as strategies that aren't trusted by their users just don't work. (I'd argue that this applies to nature's strategies as well, but I won't do that here.) Self trust is determined by an organism seeing itself as others of its immediate group or family seem to see it. If it is seen as trustworthy, that's how it will see itself. Not by any conscious usage of those terms of course, but by whatever signals all creatures have found the need to use to communicate. And all of us creatures do communicate, and need the feedback afforded by communication.

Look up the process of bacterial quorum sensing as a good example. If you haven't yet, you'll be amazed. And at the same time look up cheating in bacteria as a demonstration of their need for a mutuality of trust. No-one has attempted to explain WHY such cheaters see the need to cheat, however, but I'll try to get there.

And also try to show that all organisms need to have a sense of self, no matter how extremely limited that sense can get. They are aware of their place in however limited their discernible environment; in short it's the place that comes with a coping process that they've either come to trust instinctively, or will need to learn what else is there to trust in and survive.

Complicated? Yes. That's why we continue to evolve. The inherent tension between the trusted and the distrusted. The need to find some better balance between our cooperative and competitive strategies perhaps. Which, because of the consistency of universal change, we'll never find. It's nature's paradox, where each side must fight to win their battles, even if nether can afford to win their wars.

Here's more that I've noted about that paradoxical relation between trust and deception, where self trust will often need to involve our ability to be successfully deceptive:

"Forbidden fruit syndrome?

If in fact deception is part of our basic strategy for success, then successfully carrying out a deceptive tactic should add to our self-confidence, and perhaps, paradoxically, to our self-trust (in that we gain trust in our abilities to use these tactics). The resultant sense of satisfaction gives us pleasure, and becomes a further inducement to do something similarly deceptive in anticipation of the additional pleasure to be expected.

Pleasure then becomes the purpose of the deception in addition to the initial goals involved, and the anticipation of future pleasure while being deceptive is in itself pleasurable. It's thus conceivable that the deceptive activity that we're most successful at can be addictive, and as much through the deception involved as through the pleasure of the activity itself, whether it involves sensual pleasures, risk taking, gaming, or other commonly known addictive pursuits. And the deception can be because the activity needs to be hidden for various reasons, or because the activity itself involves a form of deception.

BUT, we also rely on self-trust as a measure of how others might judge our trustworthiness, if they could see our actual goals and methodology for attaining them. So to know that our activities would be in fact judged as characteristic of deceit would tend to erode our self-trust as well, which again seems to be an umbrella for self-confidence and self-respect. Thus we may to some extent rain on our own parade."

Yep. Conundrumable. Or simply cognitively dissonant? Nope, not a conflict of ideas. Just our most basic motivations in continual conflict as a necessary fact of life.

And I have another slew of notes made on this subject that I'll choose to pass over for now. Except for maybe these as a sample:

"How do trust strategists know when they've accomplished their purposes?" I suppose when their suspicions subside and when somehow they can feel the satisfaction we tend to feel when we attain self-trust. But actually I don't think I understand the question.

Here's one from a book on telling lies, where the author (actually a very smart guy) says, "*a liar can choose not to lie, and a praying mantis, camouflaged, is not lying.*"
I say both these assumptions are wrong .
A person whose emotional strategy is to lie will be unable to choose not to if his instincts dictate otherwise. And a mantis has intentional deception built into its strategy for survival. It is lying by concealment and also can't choose not to. It can only choose not to act on the effects of that strategy. I suppose it has to signal that "it's really me" to be trusted, although I suspect it can only communicate that to another mantis.

"*Parasites, the epitome of deceptive strategists.*" Yes. That's it on the example samples for now.

Here's what appears to be the most perplexing aspect of human deception, and as far as I know not ordinarily attributable to other species,, although it should be:

Self deception.

I'll start this with an essay that I've published on the net, which is not all bad:

"*To Thine Own Selves Be True Or Not To Be*
With regard to the enigma posed by our capacity for self-deception, the first key to the puzzle is the fact that in virtually all human cultures, deception connotes dishonesty, and dishonesty is fundamentally immoral.

A further key to be considered is that along with many animals, we humans have several higher level assessment systems, or selves, that communicate with each other, but are essentially unable to monitor the apposing assessment operations. Hence their machinations, if and when, have been de facto concealed.

And, as to the self appearing to deceive another self, immorality, as humans see it, would not have been a factor - nor become a hindrance to the evolution of our biologically deceptive functions. Primarily because these now inherent calculative strategies have been derived from largely successful results of various species' past experiences, where consequences were less dependent on the "truth" or purity of the data than on its relevance to the tactics that best addressed the problems.

And this stratagem is not so much about the invention of new data (although if need be that will happen) as the determination of that relevance by what seems to fit the situation, and the selective exclusion of what seems not to. So that in the end, the functional segments from which the accuracy of some data will be effectively concealed have almost from the start "agreed" to the arrangement.

Thus despite what we instinctively tend to feel, deception has no moral implications in that dynamic. A "self" will be deceived, but not be lied to. Because it "trusts" the deceiving self to do, or to have done, the manipulation of the data for their mutual benefit. This inducive self is not there to determine "truth" for it's own sake, but to discern whatever elements of probabilistic fact will make the system work.
(Example - to alleviate the paroxysm of fear sparked by the emotional self, the more motivated rational self will consciously select out data to reassess the probabilities of success, until everyone involved feels happy with the arrangement, and their new vision of the eventual consequences - the accuracy of which needs only in the end to be approximate.)

But then the argument will be, if the self in question knows it's being "deceived," that's really not deception - because there won't be any need or reason to accept the accuracy of the input, which had been the only purpose of the exercise. The answer is, in my view, that the "agreement" the systems have with each other calls for the manipulative act to happen when the deceiver determines it's supposed to, so that the self it happens to won't know this in advance or want to know it. Obviously it's a malleable arrangement and not all that cut and dried, as there's certainly more overt and suspicious manipulation going on within the systems, but which will largely involve the efficacy of the strategic process, rather than a question of the "motives" of the parties.
All this a lot like the "white lies" arrangements that we have with one another in most if not all human societies.

And is it this inherent inability of our internal systems to monitor and direct their operations without any form of moral compass that's led to consequences of self-deception that are self-destructive?
Especially so, the more this evolutionarily cobbled system seems to evolve itself - or the more "human" we animals have become?
And have the moral strictures within our various cultures had to evolve accordingly to counter this very problem - to deal with the weakness externally that we can't overcome internally?
And how successful will such strictures ever be, when so far we've treated this as a problem generated by some fantastical external forces, i.e., good and evil, rather than by our self-concealed internal machinery? "

Well, there are corrections that I now feel are in order, so here goes: One "self" can perhaps limit the information it shares with another, but is that hiding it or devaluing it? And in any case, we can't consciously lie to our selves without knowing we are lying and not know how to hide the knowing. So it would seem that the unconscious functions will lie to the conscious much more easily.

Additionally, our unconscious thinking is authoritative, and (as many functions are) masked by its very nature from our conscious processes. So deception in that sense is de facto occurring in the brain's systems all the time. If we're lying to ourselves, it's in an evolutionarily acceptable fashion.

The bottom line is that it's not the deceptive paradox of self versus self if we don't know we're doing it, and in any case deceptive strategies are our bread and butter, so in the end, so what? Is it an activity that should make us distrust ourselves? Perhaps, but not if we're doing it right.

Robert Trivers, evolutionary biologist and sociobiologist, wrote an article on the rightness of it in The Elements of a Scientific Theory of Self-Deception. He basically argues that we practice lying to ourselves to make us better liars when deceiving others. Perhaps, but to me that's just the half of it. And I noted that the word trust was never mentioned. Otherwise it wasn't a bad article, and a book he later wrote on the subject, The Folly of Fools, wasn't a bad book. No offense to Trivers, but I couldn't find anything in there about trust either.

Trivers had specifically argued (as in Trivers, R. L. 1981.Sociobiology and politics. In Sociobiology and Human Politics,ed. E. White. Lexington and Toronto) that *"cheating must be disguised-increasingly-even to the actor himself. As mechanisms for spotting deception become more subtle, organisms may be selected to render some facts and motives unconscious, the better to conceal deception. In the broadest sense, the organism is selected to become unconscious of some of its deception, in order not to betray, by signs of self-knowledge, the deceptions being practised"*

I must say that even though it still represents the contemporary wisdom on the subject, I find this wrong and backwards. If, as I believe, deception has been a naturally hidden practice from the start of life, organisms have had no reason to evolve the practice from a more conscious to a more unconscious strategy.

The purposes of deceptive behaviors have always been dependent on new strategies for more and more effective concealment, but not necessarily more hidden from ourselves. More likely we've simply made concealment more prevalent when we developed more separate analytical selves to complement our more animalistic ones.

And while it's accurate that we train ourselves to demonstrate belief in our own connivances, they tend to call this "acting." We still know on a different level of our selves what our more conscious selves are doing. For the sake of our survival, we have to. Been there, done that, off and on for 40 years.

So here's the realistic version of how we continuously deceive ourselves: We lie unconsciously to all and sundry endlessly and trust that we are telling them what we consciously desire to believe is the truth. In short we're being deceitful all the time to others and telling ourselves we're really not. We're persuading, manipulating, selling, concealing our own secrets, doing others good, retaliating, editing, politicizing, religicizing, you name it. But trust me, it's not necessary that we're knowingly lying.

Did I say any of that in my essay above? Not really. I believed (because I trusted) what my mostly unconscious self was telling me at the time to write, but underneath it all I had satisfied myself that all of it was probably true, and in that sense, I was continuing, even if a little bit, to lie. Because I wanted those that read the essay to trust in it, and I wanted to trust in my ability to make others trust me.

Every creature that has ever lived has similarly behaved, some much more trustworthily than others. We humans have evolved to do so in the most complicated fashion ever. And the result has been that we trust each others opinions less than any other cooperative species ever has. Yet we trust our physical selves to be safe in another's presence almost anywhere in the world that we've likely never been to before.

So we're doing the right things instinctively to personally survive, but intellectually we're as duplicitous as any animal ever was. And proud of it. Because of course, it's in our skills with duplicity that we trust.

Now if any of the above has shocked you, it was meant to. As hopefully you've sensed that, accurate or not, it was an attempt at honesty.
The most honest people can be completely wrong of course. And liars who have your best interests at heart can at least to that extent be trusted.

In any case, I want to think I've been essentially correct so far, and anything my subconscious self has selectively left out was hopefully for good reason. But I could be wrong and never know it, couldn't I. The question is, am I saying and writing whatever I've been thinking in a trustworthy fashion? In the end, it's you, the reader, who has the responsibility to decide. And not just here but with anything you hear and read. Because all of us, in one way or another, are intentionally deceiving, and acceptable or not, that's lying. OK, sermon's over.

Here's something that researchers seem to have found lately: Over-trusting oneself is better than under-trusting (accurately trusting assumedly not being possible). Which may be a lot like wishful thinking, also arguably a self-deceptive practice.

But wishes, as akin to hopes, are motivators. We give ourselves good reasons to take risks, because in the end, nothing would likely have evolved without taking what, to at least some of the participants, resulted in their individual harm and destruction.

Whether earlier life forms feared their destruction or not is another matter. Arguably the earliest social beings were trusted to fulfill their instinctively determined duties, as self trust and duty represent mutually dependent concepts, then and now. But the concept of voluntary destruction as a form of sacrifice must have been beyond them. The necessary destruction or disappearance as an individual was likely to be important as a strategic duty, and unimportant otherwise except as a setback for other aspects of their cooperative strategies.

But life on the whole has obviously survived, and risk takers among us have survived accordingly. Some more than others, of course, but risk taking as an inherently dangerous practice not only continues to exist but prospers. It has become a strategic process that we trust. And beating what we've perceived to be the odds becomes instinctively exciting. Risky behavior, with the expected dopamine rush as the motivator, becomes its own reward. Pleasure in the doing makes the goal worth getting, as some say.

(It also occurs to me that love is a bit like risky over-trusting, and jealously, a bit like risky suspicioning. But I'll need another book and much more research to cover these and other emotional aspects of the trust - distrust - deception spectrum.)

Sense of self. Some refer to this as necessary for having a "theory of mind." Which according to Wikipedia is in turn the ability to attribute mental states—beliefs, intents, desires, pretending, knowledge, etc.—to oneself and others and to understand that others have beliefs, desires and intentions that are different from one's own. So my question is, do life forms need a mere sense of self to be deceptive, or do they need to have added some version of a theory of mind? Or if in fact all life forms have had to learn that others are deceptive from the get-go, then haven't they always possessed some version of self-knowledge and of "others-knowledge" from the start?

The following should indicate that single celled bacteria in any case had most likely acquired those essential attributes of life's intelligence from their inception:

From a Scientific American article, again about quorum sensing:
"As its moniker suggests, quorum sensing describes the ways in which bacteria determine how many of them there are in the vicinity. If enough are present (a quorum), they can get down to business or up to mischief. For instance, millions of bioluminescent bacteria might decide to emit light simultaneously so that their host, a squid, can glow--perhaps to distract predators and escape. Or salmonella bacteria might wait until their hordes have amassed before releasing a toxin to sicken their host; if the bacteria had acted as independent assassins rather than as an army, the immune system most likely would have wiped them out."

My comments from my notes re their strategies were as follows:
"Risk level for an attack on their host decreases with added strength in numbers, so their apparent potential for danger is masked (more passive deception) and they change to attack mode when signals show their numbers are sufficient to overcome resistance in their prey - which in turn was deceived by their seeming harmlessness into lack of preparedness or suspicion of the deceptive capacity inherent in the bacteria. This lack of suspicion corresponds to a greater degree of trust and tolerance than would have been the case without the masking strategy.

So what makes deception a primary part of the strategy rather than a secondary aspect? Deception had to be there first before any following efforts could have succeeded. Suspicion of deception can only be overcome by passive deception - a masking of true "intentions" (de facto intent as it were) to induce a higher level of trust.

And the mutual trust practiced by the grouping of similar bacteria was a necessary element in allowing the deceptive strategy to work against their mutual prey. (One of the many permutations of the way trust and deception work hand in hand as it were - and paradoxically when you consider that trust is dependent on deception for its very existence.)

And yet we are dealing with life forms that have no brains or known nervous systems to calculate how, when, and where to use these maneuvers or formations. But they have nevertheless evolved to automatically probe, signal, and react to signals in complicated ways that assure the odds of their survival will increase more when these methods are the result of that stimuli than the odds would otherwise have favored them in their particular environment."

I'm no longer using the word "automatic" in this context but otherwise that sums my present feelings up. Automatic is what some biologists still use to support the mechanistic theories that bacteria were simply reactive to stimuli, somewhat akin to machines, or to our own autonomic nervous systems. But clearly they appear to use the same type of intelligent planning that we do. Less conceptually abstract, perhaps, but on the other hand they can make their own toxins, and routinely evolve their functional properties and systems to meet new challenges from their environments, and especially those from us, Doing things that, if we can also do, we've likely had to learn to do from them.

Fine. I've reached the point where, should I have kicked off now, I've got the main part of my thesis out there for the modest ages. But, hey, there's more!

Let's try to tackle the biggest mystery of all.

Intelligence.

From a Newsweek article,
Our Bodies, Our Fears
Feb 23, 2003
"The brain is not just a thinking machine. It's a biological adaptation, designed to promote survival in the environments where it evolved. As neuroscientist Steven Hyman of the National Institutes of Mental Health observes, "Survival depends on the ability of an organism to respond to threat or reward, and predict the circumstances under which they are likely

to occur." The brain structures that handle that job evolved long before the neocortex (the seat of conscious awareness), and they easily override it. The "emotional brain," as LeDoux calls this web of ancient circuitry, is highly attuned to signs of potential danger. And through a process known as fear conditioning, it can readily learn to perceive a mundane stimulus as a warning sign."

Except that, to me, this is not entirely accurate, as I've noted earlier. We need more than a mundane stimulus to warn us against deceptive practices. We need intelligent strategies that can only be intelligently fashioned.
So whether or not the brain is "just a thinking machine," where did the thinking that made it work come from? Organisms, when life began, supposedly had nothing known as brains to start with. How can an organism without, or even with, a brain learn *anything* without having, as a requisite, the minimum of intelligence required to learn to think at all?

Or to put it differently, how would our earth's original organisms, that haven't yet evolved an ability to feel some equivalence of pain, learn without initial intelligence to avoid the things that only later could have contributed to the evolution of sensations as warnings that the organism might be about to be eaten?

We have had to assume that organisms did learn, although the general opinion has been that they learned to work with evolutionary changes that somehow accidentally occurred outside of any direct connection with that organism's experience. Which fit in nicely with a belief from Darwin's day that organism's weren't intelligent from the start. (Although Darwin in particular tended to have ideas otherwise.)

Yet even if these organisms learned to profit from accidents, they still had to have intelligence to learn at all. Few of us seem to have seen the problem there. If organisms did start life with enough intelligence to learn, they wouldn't need to wait for accidents to amend their behaviors. And especially since they were single celled creatures, learned behaviors would have been much easier to replicate by cell division than by the accidental evolutionary processes that subsequently came to be in vogue. But if they had no intelligence to start with, how did they learn any of the things that allowed them to be designated as alive at all?

The essence of all life is the ability to make choices.that non-life supposedly can't make. All evolutionists agree that one way or another, life has responsibility for the success of its own choices. Most of them know this takes some bit of strategic intelligence. Some of us know that life had to always have that bit. We don't know at this time where it came from. But if we didn't just pull it out of our accidental hats, intelligently strategic processes have been out there somewhere for a long time before we living things had got here.

Ordinarily, the theory of evolution is not so much concerned with the genesis of life as with the mechanisms that caused, or allowed, it to evolve. But an auxiliary hypothesis of motivating causes, such as I'm proposing, which is concerned with the mechanisms of life from its inception, has to touch on the nature of those mechanisms' genesis as well.

Because again, in any such examination of the process, we should need to consider the element of purpose. And especially the degree to which life forms will have created their own purposes for being, rather than the degree, if any, that this purpose has been thrust upon them. And if intelligence has been thrust upon us, what purpose was served by that event, and what purposes might be more intelligently acquired by us for serving that intelligence intelligently.

So let me define intelligence more specifically as the ability to use the trial and error process to solve predictive problems. Which fits quite well with my proposals here that life's strategies are made to serve predictive purposes. Simply put, they make use of a complicated algorithmic process to examine the environmental patterns from their sensory input and compare these moving "mental" holographs to the trusted patterns they've either memorized from previous experiences or been instinctively provided. (Instincts that were also derived from experiences of some organisms back down the line of heritability). Intelligently looking for what's there and happening that shouldn't be, or not there and happening that should.

From this information, they use their own trusted probability scales to select from their particular set of pretested optional behaviors that the patterns found can be expected to fit, and send signals to their motor apparatus that will trigger the appropriate actions in response. Not a process that's been conferred upon these organisms by accident.

From a paper by David Sloan Wilson Departments of Biology and Anthropology Binghamton University on Evolutionary Volutionary Social Constructivism. (The same Wilson previously referred to above.) Re the concept of behavioral flexibility, also called phenotypic plasticity:

"No organism is so simple that it is instructed by its genes to "do x". Even bacteria and protozoa are genetically endowed with a set of if-then rules of the form "do x in situation 1", "do y in situation 2" and so on. These rules enable organisms to do the right thing at the right time, not only behaviorally but physiologically and morphologically. The literature on non-humans is full of wonderful examples of caterpillars that look like twigs in spring and leaves in summer, fish that grow streamlined bodies in the absence of predators but flattened bodies in their presence to exceed the gape of their jaws, frog eggs designed to hatch prematurely at the approach of a snake, salamanders that morph into big-jawed cannibals when food becomes short, and on and on. In all of these cases, information from the environment is combined with a set of predetermined if-then rules to determine the structure and behavior of the organism, much as your tax-preparation software branches off in different directions depending upon the information that it prompts you for."

This seems to fit fairly well with what I've described But I'd add that more than having rules of the form "do x in situation 1", "do y in situation 2" and so on, such algorithms, and especially with humans, are multi strategic, with additional rules like "do x strategy in response to y strategy, and y strategy in response to z strategy, etc. And within Y strategy, consider options/tactics a and b, etc.

Life forms can put a seemingly massive amount of information in what seems like an infinitesimally small space. Note also that while some insects, such as the ants, have strategies that are persistently instinctive, they nevertheless find purposes and ways to use them quite intelligently. Intuitive reactions of all species are very far from automatic.

Each species may have particular scenarios with symbols of strategically important entities to be wary of, such as (in our case) snakes and such. And these fears could carry over when species adapt to new environments or branch off, but more importantly, the strategies themselves will be evolved to encompass new varieties of strategic targets. Hence we humans don't need the many thousands, if not millions, of alleged "if-then" modules that we've supposedly, as some propose, inherited from primitive man, etc. (But evolutionary psychologists are evolving too.)

We and other organisms, from bacteria on up the multicellular lines, learn and adapt our own strategies continually from more present day experiences. We examine the expected with trust, and examine the unexpected with distrust. These purposes have been well served by that old trial and error process, which has become the backbone of all our developing intelligences.

But of course we still don't know exactly how the experiences that change our expectations are then transmitted as instinctive "knowledge" to future generations. More on that later, perhaps. What we can be confident of now is that the intelligence found in our universe evolves.

Empathy is then our next subject. Intelligence evolves, but life wouldn't have evolved intelligently without empathy. This is also a function that earlier forms of life supposedly wouldn't have evolved without a "theory of mind" to go with it. But again there has probably been the sort of mutual sensing of another's purposes, and their expectations concerning ours, from the time life made choices in a social situation. Which all life was required always to participate in, whatever the adaptive strategy being used to survive and replicate. We likely could not have adapted strategies at all without empathy, and not made use of our new skills to evolve our cultures - and cultures to evolve our new intelligence - all being fundamentally dependent on each other.

Empathy facilitates trust. If you can sense what another is thinking or feeling, you can then have confidence in your ability to trust what you feel, rather than guess what the others motives or intentions are. And just as importantly you can give them a reliable way to judge what your feelings are and show them your own trustworthiness as well.

It's a mutually beneficial predictability mechanism, essential to cooperation within and also between species, assuming that cooperation is the goal. Empathy does not necessarily lead to sympathy when our cooperative needs are absent. Which then can lead to a game of concealing such feelings when needing trust is superseded by some more competitive necessity.

Empathy makes it hard to outright lie and not get caught at it through your "body language." But since we have learned to use our unconscious processes so routinely to deceive, it's also relatively easy for the empathetic in a similar culture to "acceptably" deceive each other. So that empathy in those cases ironically facilitates deception as well. For an example, look up the meaning of affinity fraud, where those of the same culture lie successfully to each other by assuring all and sundry that they aren't. All involved having learned their particular cultural game of concealing their true feelings well.

Lying among monkeys for example is supposed by some animal researchers to show that they have learned to think about what others are thinking. Learned to utilize that aspect of empathy supposedly. But more likely deception via the empathetic process has long been an instinctive strategy, learned and improved over time, and adapted by changes in circumstance and culture.

So perhaps what the monkeys have learned is the strategy that we've also learned better, one that tells us the signs to look for if and when the other reacts to our strategy with a counter strategy. - not knowing via empathy what another actually thinks as much as knowing what he should and likely will be using as a counter strategy.

Simply put, you lie to obtain or maintain trust re your intentions, they find a reason to suspect your motives, you spot that they have "doubts" by their postures, you try to reassure them, or in one alternative defend yourself from retaliation, or just give up the ploy. Examine your own actions carefully and you might find you use empathy to your advantage daily to successfully (or so it seems) deceive your companions in a fashion appropriate to the situation, and acceptable by the game playing rules of your culture.

And yes, experts such as primatologist Frans B. M. de Waal believe that monkeys, chimps, and other higher primates have genuine empathy, the ability to imagine themselves in another animal's place. And that may be the first step in the evolution of morality, as De Waal writes in The Evolution of Empathy: "We are so used to empathy that we take it for granted, yet it is essential to human society as we know it. Our morality depends on it: How could anyone be expected to follow the golden rule without the capacity to mentally trade places with a fellow human being?"

The problem is of course that there are no strategies in life that have successfully evolved by following any one particular rule, and with empathy as our tool, we have more easily evolved to follow other and less friendly rules in dealing with our fellow humans.

And again, these less friendly practices didn't start with us. Chimps, as pointed out above, may use their empathic skills for "good," but also to manipulate others for "bad." Talents which require mental sophistication, as some have put it. But while animal researchers often seem surprised that animals use deceptive strategies similar to ours, they should look into the strategies of ocean creatures for some real surprises. And particularly at cephalopods. They've got us land animals beat deceptively by miles.

However, let me give a more interesting example from my notes of how some other land animals deceive (or think they are deceiving) their prospective sexual partners. Each partner making use of empathy in the bargain. Or perhaps more accurately, in the bargaining.

Excerpts from a New York Times article, May 24, 2010, By Sindya Bhanoo Male Antelopes Scare Partners Into Sex:

During mating season, a male topi antelope will try to keep females in heat from leaving his territory by pretending that a predator might be in the area, When a female appears to be leaving, the male will run in front of her, freeze in place, stare in the direction that she is going and snort loudly. Typically, that snort means that a predatory lion or cheetah was spotted, but in this case the male is faking it.

"He doesn't look at the female. He takes a rigid stance exactly as if there were a predator there," said Jakob Bro-Jorgensen, a research fellow at the University of Liverpool who led the study. Dr. Bro-Jorgensen, who studied the behavior of hundreds of topi antelopes in the Masai Mara National Reserve, said the males acted this way time after time.

Although scientists have observed males deceiving other males to gain access to mates, this is the first finding of a male duping his own sexual partner, Dr. Bro-Jorgensen said. Hearing the snort, the female antelope generally retreats back into the male's territory, where he will attempt to mate with her right away. Females mate with many males each season, and it would seem that they might catch on after a while. But getting fooled does not have much of a downside, while ignoring what might be a real warning could be deadly.

"It's too dangerous to take the chance," Dr. Bro-Jorgensen said.

Asked whether this sort of behavior might occur in humans, Dr. Bro-Jorgensen said he did not know, but "We are masters of deception, so of course you can speculate."

My comment in my notes: *Amazing that they don't recognize that there must be an evolutionary advantage to this strategy that didn't start with antelopes. And hasn't stopped with us.*

So it seems clear from all of this that deception has to have always been an integral part of any animal's information processing. And survival has to depend on organisms learning what their deceptive dangers are through some of them having survived such danger, and these survivors having a rudimentary capacity for recognizing how that danger adversely effected the non-survivors.

There has to be a semblance of memory and of an ability to make simple analogies, and to recognize the similarities between other organisms and themselves - in order to have the rudiments of what we now call empathy.

The organisms with the best of these inceptive capabilities will tend to survive and pass on these qualities. We refer to the benefits of these experiences as instinctive knowledge. Yet it is knowledge that was clearly passed on by other organisms, So we should understand that instincts have somehow been the results of all our past experiences, even if at present we don't completely understand the mechanisms through which much of this has been accomplished.

However, some of these instinctive lessons must be passed on by each species' version of an external social culture. But in the case of empathy we seem to have evolved an additional internal channel that has more of an individually determined character than that of the socially determined behaviors it helps us to detect. As I said earlier, we don't know all the answers as to why and how, but hopefully we're asking better questions.

And I haven't talked off what happens when an animal or human seems to have been made or born without the individual ability to use the empathetic process. Which would include, in particular, human psychopaths. But this is one form of disorder among many that run the gamut of a huge list of mental illnesses. Although I've spent years dealing with the problems that many of these people cause, this book was not meant to do justice to that subject. As I keep saying, maybe next time.

But my experience has convinced me at this moment that all of these conditions are facilitated in one way or another by deceptive processes and mental sufferers make use of the same processes as the sane, either voluntarily or involuntarily, to try to survive. As survival by the more normal process of knowing when to reasonably trust, and when not to, is largely unavailable to them.

Culture. Let's focus a bit more on that. Without it, we wouldn't have empathy, and without empathy, our deceptive strategies would not have as effectively evolved, and if not that, our intelligence would not have been fit to make a decent human. Of course none of that should truly be at issue, as without some form of culture, there'd likely be no life to be concerned about at all.

Culture from the start has told us what to trust, and then what not to trust, and the more our cultures have evolved, they've told us when and how, and even why, to lie. Acceptably, that is.

Culture consists of, in large part, and for each species it applies to, a set of mutually understood rules as to both overt and covert acts that are or are not seen as acceptable, and of the rules by which the unacceptable are to be dealt with. And the acceptable rewarded, I should add. More importantly, cultures assist in the heritability of the characteristics that each evolving species has learned and acquired from a "tipping point" combination of their individual experiences. Each of their cultures provide the platform for their behaviors' strategic developments and the purposes they'll have the need and ability to acquire, and in addition are the mechanism that "spreads the word" that accelerates the individual acquisitions of these acquired strategies "instinctively."

And even more importantly, if I'm correct in my initial hypothesis, cultures will have contributed in particular to the rapid evolution of the ways we have applied life's strategic foundations to allow the evolution of any of its forms that could have a hope of surviving at all.

But lets talk a bit about how the acceptable and unacceptable are often seen by different people in different walks and different places as very similar behaviors that in those particular aspects are very different.

I like to think of the 18th century philosopher, Immanuel Kant, as offering one of the best examples of the conflict between those who believe cultures have ideals from some universal loft to live up to, and those who believe ideals should defer to the circumstances that we can realistically trust down here on the different ground where each of us were more suitably selected to stand.

Kant offered what has been referred to as the Categorical Imperative, and did so in rebuttal of what, at the time, was known as the Doctrine of Mental Reservation. Mental reservation is a form of deception which is not an outright lie. It was supported in the moral theology at the time as a way to fulfill obligations both to tell the truth and to keep secrets from those not entitled to know them. (Wikipedia has more on the subject which I invite you to read, but not right now.)

But according to Kant (and Wikipedia), human beings occupied a special place in creation, and morality could be summed up in one ultimate commandment of reason, or imperative, from which all duties and obligations derive. To quote from Wikipedia:

"Kant asserted that lying, or deception of any kind, would be forbidden under any interpretation and in any circumstance. In Grounding, Kant gives the example of a person who seeks to borrow money without intending to pay it back. This is a contradiction because if it were a universal action, no person would lend money anymore as he knows that he will never be paid back. The maxim of this action, says Kant, results in a contradiction in conceivability (and thus contradicts perfect duty). With lying, it would logically contradict the reliability of language. If it is universally acceptable to lie, then no one would believe anyone and all truths would be assumed to be lies. The right to deceive could also not be claimed because it would deny the status of the person deceived as an end in himself. And the theft would be incompatible with a possible kingdom of ends. Therefore, Kant denied the right to lie or deceive for any reason, regardless of context or anticipated consequences."

But then to quote Wikipedia as to the objections of the philosopher, Arthur Schopenhauer:
"Schopenhauer's criticism of the Kantian philosophy expresses doubt concerning the absence of egoism in the Categorical Imperative."
"According to Schopenhauer, Kant's Categorical Imperative:
- *Redundantly repeats the ancient command: "don't do to another what you don't want done to you."*
- *Is egoistic because its universality includes the person who both gives and obeys the command.*
- *Is cold and dead because it is to be followed without love, feeling, or inclination, but merely out of a sense of duty."*

Obviously I have to agree with Schopenhauer. Although I wouldn't offer my complete trust to either of these once influential men, Schopenhauer's ideas were seen in general as more realistic, and as a consequence more influential with the people that made the more significant changes to their cultures. Not that the machinations of the influential were trusted by the public in general, but somewhat paradoxically, their philosophies were seen by their supporters as fountains of the best advice. And those who turned to Schopenhauer may have got the better of it, but even to this day, the people that look for sustenance from Kant are a surprisingly insatiable group.

In a way, both these men's ideas were representative of the punitive attitudes in their prevailing cultures, prompting assumptions that somehow deception in general was against our human natures. And thus the logical "codification" encouraged by these (and many other) historical philosophies engrained their differing yet authoritative assumptions deeper into the cultural milieux. Acceptable deceptions that were classified as not truly lying persist in all our cultures to this day; protecting us from feeling that our honest intentions could be deceptive at all, and certainly not dangerously so.

All of this aided by the instinctive lessons inherited from our (supposedly) more superstitious ancestors, which some would call their "culturally preserved" assumptions. Over time many of these instinctive "lessons" can and will turn out to be seriously misguided, driving us quite nuts in our nearest futures, great portions of our cultures calling out for wars and jihads, etc., etc. (I'll need another book for that.)

I'm tempted to say more about Kant as the great rationalizer, but not here. And if I'm not mistaken, Kant conceded he likely wouldn't act in practice as he'd recommended in theory. And in any case, ironically, the distinctions in these systems don't make much difference in the end. Since if not entirely acceptable in Kant's day for Kantians to knowingly lie, it would be acceptable today in almost every culture to lie to a determined murderer about the location of the prey that you may or may not have helped to hide. And in the majority of these cultures as well, it could earn you a badge of honor to resist all threats and torture to 'persuade' you otherwise. Honor, by the way, representing near to the highest form of trust in almost all of our societies.

And if you haven't noticed, we've now had examples of acceptable lying that we don't knowingly admit are necessary lies, as well as lies that are acceptable because we knowingly admit they're necessary lies. And either way, the wars that are best conducted by lies of all types continue. Perhaps it's not the lies that are the problem, but the inability to trust each others versions of the truth.

But then what is the bigger picture of this culture that preserves the rules that we learn and somewhat fruitlessly expect ourselves to live by? In my possibly unorthodox view it's the collection of everything that all life forms have discovered as informative and found ways to communicate to each other, as well as to their internal machinery, that has been preserved in and outside of these creatures since life of any sort began, both here on earth and possibly somewhere long before that. And of things that non-life has found ways to inform us of as well - the lessons of the universe that we have evolved to find ways to access and make as useful as we can.

How then does culture supposedly differ from species to species, from habitat to habitat, social group to social group, and family to family? Perhaps only in that all these rather arbitrary groupings are parts of the great whole of the world's learning that each species has been given or achieved their often very different ways and means of access to. And perhaps that's just a flight of my fantasy, but of course I doubt it..

Well then where does this great conglomeration of culture stuff reside? What I was intending to say earlier was that it's not floating in the air somewhere (as some still feel our evolutionary selective processes are), but within our individual memories as we live, and in what we've left for others to remember when we've gone. But I knew intuitively as soon as I started to write it that this was wrong. Because our culture is floating, metaphorically, in our environment everywhere.

Culture is the product of our biological learning processes that waits to communicate with us in our adaptive, and adapted to, environments. In the parts we have caused to fit our needs, our harrowed fields, our living structures, our roads, bridges, as well as in the domesticated animals we've used to build things, to travel on, to produce as well as furnish us our food, and to become in many ways our closest friends. And culture's in our arts, our architecture, paintings, sculptures, literature, music and whatever else you'll spot that I've left out.

Which some might say include the remnants of the cultures we've destroyed. Which is to also say that whatever we've abandoned or forgotten has nevertheless become essential to our present. But can we call that "culture" which we can no longer take a lesson from? Probably not. There are endless forms of existing cultures that most of us will never have the desire or the chance to learn from as it is.

And what we learn in any case are more sophisticated ways to benefit from the strategic processes of our lives that we trust, as well as the deceptive tactics of these same strategies that may, ironically, protect us from the similar strategic forays of the distrusted. (Again, a reminder that trust is not necessarily good or honest, and deception is not necessarily evil or dishonest, which hopefully I'll have demonstrated by the time I'm done here.)

So as it's been my contention here and elsewhere that "all evolution is the proximate result of the entity involved reacting strategically to its experience," I'll try at this point to show further how the evolution of our apparently antagonistic strategies have served life's purposes from the time they were first experiencing the uniqueness of the problems to be met and solved on earth. If they had a choice in the matter, of course.

I've chosen bacteria as the life forms that should best do that job for me, as they are likely among our first users of these earthbound strategies, and the first users of cultural communication to make these strategies work, and more importantly apply the totality of the learning gained to the process of evolving on this planet effectively. As it's fairly safe to say that among the bacteria that live today are some of those that were alive then, and have been alive for more than three billion years.

And I'll let some of the best scientists that work with bacteria and evaluate their behaviors speak for me as follows:

Excerpts from Bacteria Harnessing Complexity, By Eshel Ben Jacob, Yakir Aharonov and Yoash Shapira, Tel Aviv University:

"Bacteria, being the first form of life on earth, had to devise ways to synthesize the complex organic molecules required for life. They are able to reverse the spontaneous course of entropy increase and convert high-entropy inorganic substances into low- entropy life-sustaining molecules. Three and a half billion years have passed, and the existence of higher organisms depends on this unique bacterial know-how. Even for us, with all our scientific knowledge and technological advances, the ways bacteria solve this fundamental requirement for life is still a mystery"

"According to this picture, new features collectively emerge during biotic self-organization on every level, from the internal cellular gel to the whole colony. The cells thus assume newly co-generated traits and abilities that are not explicitly stored in the genetic information of the individuals. For example, bacteria cannot genetically store all the information required for creating the colonial patterns. In the new picture, they don't need to, since the required information is cooperatively generated as self-organization proceeds by bacterial communication, informatics and self-plasticity capabilities. Thus, the bacteria need only have genetically stored the guidelines for producing these capabilities and using them to generate new information as required."

And this:
"if we keep in mind that each bacterium has an internal structure with high levels of flexibility and inherent variations, these observations suggest that the patterns are not arbitrary but involve some internal sophisticated means of regulation and control. So, for example, upon replication, the new cells will immediately have the proper internal gene expression states to fit the colonial behavior."

I suggest that anyone who wants to see the evidence that supports the above contentions should read the complete paper, as well as other papers I've referenced from scientists such as James Shapiro. I won't claim however that they support my hypothesis as it pertains to the trust and distrust dynamic. My assumption at present is that few to none of our scientists or philosophers of science have needed to consider it at all. Hopefully I can change that, as I expect that these ideas, if to flourish, will need all the help they can get.

But right now I want to comment on the meaning of "colonial behavior," as noted at the end of the above quotes from the 'Bacteria Harnessing Complexity' paper.

Colonial behavior equals culturally communicated and shared behavioral rules and tactics. Organisms of the same species gathering to form a community to serve the same collective purposes for survival. They cooperate to find food, to protect themselves from prey as well as to, at times, collectively prey on other such communities.

These colonies are not restricted to single celled organisms, as these interdependent communities are formed by everything from penguins to people. The differences are in the cultures of each colony which retain the lessons from experience that have formed and reformed their collections of behavioral options. The strategies that are not only selectable by choice, but are used to control every aspect of their operations, as well as help them engineer their own construction. And remarkably, by their cultures of communication, sharable by all in each respective colony.

All of these activities motivated by the need to find avenues for life's satisfactions that they can most likely trust, and avoid the avenues that they suspect will do them in, if that trust is misplaced.

But we've talked some about trust within each species having followed the same general strategies from the get-go, but not much about the inter species function of trust, of which the best examples might be found in how animals react to domestication, and their new human masters react to them in turn.

Inter species trust, culturally determined or instinctive in the wild, has to change when one group finds ways to dominate and use the other. Are the more instinctive suspicions of each group involved in domestication's master-slave relationship alleviated by what becomes a cultural necessity?

Isn't there a cultural adaptation at this point? And in time some instinctive change to follow? We'll try to see.

If trust versus distrust strategies have been intelligently and culturally adapted by all species, then species that must adapt their strategies in new ways to each other, must adapt their cultures to each other as well. Cultures that of course can't think, but reside in thinking individuals, whose intelligence will continue to contribute to all cultures they may come to have a stake in.

Will the more complex of the cultures that have in effect evolved a third culture between them, remain the better at deceiving the less complex in the end? In the long term, perhaps yes. In the short term, not necessarily.

Domestication can give us the best example of how all cultures are altered by their interplay, and how this interplay will contribute to the evolution of each species' learned and instinctive strategies in the bargain.

Note to begin with that offspring of wild species are not necessarily distrusting of other species when first born. The young of predators may instinctively sense the natures of their traditional prey - but not know the tactics used to capture them. And not know to fear the defensive potential of their prospective victims, or the offensive potential of those who in turn may prey on them.

We learn this when, for example, we take young animals such as lion cubs to raise in our own culture's compounds without contact with others of their species. We note on those occasions that these animals (with some notable exceptions) will tend to provisionally trust us, and will learn that it's in their interest not to have us distrust them.

They learn to obey the rules that our culture has for them, rather than the customs that their essential natures had intended to be theirs. Because of course they had evolved to survive as self sufficient operators in their parents' culture, and not as either slaves or dependents of the reigning members of our human culture.

Further, as we see with domesticated species such as dogs, the behaviors they will come to learn as a group in our human cultures will in the main be taught to them by members of their own domesticated species, and in time with the help and lessons of experience, some of these newer strategies will override their earlier instinctive strategies and become heritable as well. Check out the evolutionary history of dogs as the best evidence.

Dogs in particular will have learned from both their human masters and other domesticated dogs - good learners selected and bad learners culled - to trust and obey their masters in the end. Sheep, goats, cows, horses, raised for different purposes, will still have similar domestication histories

Some may object at this point that neoteny, also called juvenilization, is a more crucial factor in domestication, where dogs are bred for size instead of behavior. But in fact they have had to select for neotenous behavioral traits to get those unusually smaller sizes.

We're always brought back to that question when discussing any type of evolutionary change: The form or its strategy, which one evolves the other? And it may seem a lot like the "chicken or the egg first" conundrum. But my answer is that the chicken can decide to reconstruct its eggs. The egg however can't decide to reconstruct its chickens. Where the intelligence has to come from is always the key.

In the end, some animals will have adapted by responding to a trainer's kindness, and the others in response to their cruelty. So that even with domestication, the trust discovered between the domesticated and their masters in some human cultures will differ markedly from that found in some others.

Which for me is evidence as to how different cultures may affect some differences in a domesticated animal's overridden (or "overwritten") instincts. Trust by some animals of humans in the crueler cultures has been long mixed with fear, but for the same breeds of animals in other human cultures, trust seems not to have been tempered by such cruel and deceptive tactics.

An article in National Geographic, July 2012, Vanishing Languages, helps to provide an excellent example of how, and to some degree why, these relationships can differ. The article was not written as much to examine cultures as to examine their languages at risk. Words and their meanings to be lost included those used by the Mongush on the Siberian taiga, in the Republic of Tuva, part of the Russian Federation.

One word suggested by students there was khoj özeeri, the Tuvan method of killing a sheep. To quote from the article:

"If slaughtering livestock can be seen as part of humans' closeness to animals, khoj özeeri represents an unusually intimate version. Reaching through an incision in the sheep's hide, the slaughterer severs a vital artery with his fingers, allowing the animal to quickly slip away without alarm, so peacefully that one must check its eyes to see if it is dead.
In the language of the Tuvan people, khoj özeeri means not only slaughter but also kindness, humaneness, a ceremony by which a family can kill, skin, and butcher a sheep, salting its hide and preparing its meat and making sausage with the saved blood and cleansed entrails so neatly that the whole thing can be accomplished in two hours (as the Mongushes did this morning) in one's good clothes without spilling a drop of blood. Khoj özeeri implies a relationship to animals that is also a measure of a people's character. As one of the students explained, "If a Tuvan killed an animal the way they do in other places"—by means of a gun or knife—"they'd be arrested for brutality."

Note for my purposes here that this animal seems to have complete trust in these human masters, and they honor that trust by deceiving it as painlessly as possible in the killing of it. A somewhat hidden reason for having given that animal life, although not necessarily a bargain it would knowingly have made. Both species, sheep and human, in their own way have benefitted from the one needing to deceive the other. Perhaps as we, the more intelligent of our living forms, nevertheless have accepted a bargain with nature that requires our eventual death in exchange for being given at least the temporary use of life.

We've noted a relationship to animals here that's also a measure of the Tuvan people's character. I've learned as well that Tuvans have an animistic culture, believing there are souls and spirits, not only in humans, but also in all other animals, plants, and rocks. They also, according to the National Geographic article, believe that "the past is ahead of them while the future lies behind." The children look to the future, "but it's behind them, not yet seen."

Try thinking about that with a "western cultured" mind. You feel that it somehow has the ring of truth, but why? Perhaps it's the sense that, while we feel that we make life happen, they feel that life makes them happen. The future is pulling us and pushing them.

My guess is they don't fear that future, not being culturally disposed to distrust the present. But what does it mean for the past to be ahead of them? Good memories and few regrets? Or expectations that the future will repeat the past? Clearly, they have more trust than distrust in each other, their animals and their environment. They seem not to expect the future to surprise them or betray them. Trusting from experience that it won't. Their culture not seeing that as the future's purpose.

I could go on to show more ways the world's various and sundry species adapt their cultures in concert with other species they more commonly do deceptive battle with, but I won't. My intent was to demonstrate that it happens, and I'm more interested now in showing how our cultures affect our evolutionary strategies in general. I don't have the time, or space, and certainly not the present knowledge to go much further into that series of particulars. Maybe in the next book if I'm lucky.

I had this comment in my notes that might be appropriate to add here: *"It would seem that we grow into different species by adding options to our survival strategies that help them fit our new experiences. Whether we ever completely erase our earlier acquired instincts is doubtful. We'd have to completely alter the basis of our strategies to do so, and just as we carry remnants of our foundational forms, it seems we'd need to retain the elements of our foundational strategies as well. Especially if we'd have to erase all remnants of these strategies from our cultures in the bargain."*

So let that serve as a transition to a question that some of you may ask: How can a culture, for example, play a part in its individuals finding ways to strategically reconstruct their species' physical forms, and then pass on the instructions culturally rather than the accepted method of having those newer forms and functions inherited genetically by its children, especially when there simply won't be anything near the "accidental" changes to selectively affect enough of that culture's other children in that same time period to modify the physical aspects of this comprehensive evolutionary change?

Well maybe because our physical forms aren't all that accidentally changed in any case. And I don't know how any of the various culture's members have found the physical means to alter their forms genetically to begin with. Although of course, as to bacterial cultures and the like, they seem to do it one way or another all the time. And so must we.

It seems that with the communicative advantages of cultures, if at the very least one individual devises a particular strategy from experience, then another with the same experience can be more easily influenced to copy it. And this sharing of experiences for mutual progress will certainly accelerate the evolutionary process, but can still take many generations to create heritable physical and mental changes in a colonial or cultural group. Especially where multicellular individuals are involved.

But the standard evolutionary theories tell us that cultures play little or no part, since neither do the experiences they claim to share, and we're assured that nature's accidents are doing this instead for all concerned. Except obviously not in anywhere close to the same length of time that bacteria and many other of life's species have recently been observed to do it. Thus, to me, offering perhaps one of the more unlikely scenarios ever by some of the more intelligent members of our human species.

All theories for example accept that the organisms in the end do the actual construction by themselves. Are we then supposed to believe that the constructive engineering process is all done by accident, in spite of the evidence that all life forms are constructed at least somewhat intelligently by something. Creationists of course will tell you that some Gods have done it. Dawkinsists (another word for neo-Darwinists) still tell us we select from random accidents that have eventually somehow selected proper changes for our forms through causing defects, non-purposively, in our genes. Because, they say, we've never been intelligent enough to "design" ourselves, even when for ages we've observed our own bodies rebuilding various parts of us every day.

Mindless structures of course can't act to build themselves at all. But can't strategies that direct behaviors be expected to direct them to behave as builders? And what is it that assesses and selects the elements from nature that can be tried and tested as useable materials? Because if we have evolved to use the trial and error process, which requires that we use these errors to our best advantage, aren't we allowed to make intelligent use of accidents via the same or similar process that nature has supposedly been doing things all this time by accident?

Instead, the standard theories inform us oddly that our intelligent powers were given their advantages by nature's accidents, rather than give any credence at all to the more sophisticated conception that such accidents are clearly taken advantage of by life's intelligence. (Which of course must be a form of nature's intelligence as well, no?)

From my notes: *"Behavioral strategies have to anticipate the advantage to be taken of both the intentional and accidental. Accident on the other hand has no capacity to take advantage of behavior. It cannot acquire motivation or incentive – it can't do more than serve our capabilities there. Accidents that do otherwise are misdefined as accidental."*

And further, as to learning and evolving ways to build ourselves, there are recently published studies, interestingly, where bacteria have been found to physically pass everything they've learned strategically to their immediate descendants. And do it as a function of their replicatory systems, which are primarily cell duplication processes. Multicellular organisms apparently can't do that, as they don't replicate by division. They have needed to use the communicative forms of cultures for that process.

Assuming of course they wouldn't have evolved from single cell to multi-cell if they hadn't found a way to transfer strategies, and we know of course that they can transfer instinctive strategies to their progeny. It's the newly learned behavioral strategies that must supposedly, from a Dawkinsist viewpoint anyway, be relearned each generation.

Although it seems that newly discovered epigenetic processes may be doing for the rest of us what duplication has done for bacteria. None of which we fully need to know to understand how trust was parried by distrust and deception to motivate the whole ball of wax, but it's interesting to discover bit by bit how all things have actually evolved to deal with those competing elements of our motivating forces.

Bacteria still use their original cell division methods, but run their cooperative ventures by culture-wide communicative methods. And they do these things in a very large part for us, the humans, since we have more bacterial cells that functionally operate within and for our bodies than those of our own origin that have furnished our human instinctive behavior patterns and our human functional apparatus for all varieties of our human and microbial cells to further use in constructing our collective bodies.

But I make no claim to knowing exactly what does what to which and why. I think however that I know something of the nature of our own strategic purposes, How we've physically evolved to use these chosen strategies is much more important than accepting the prevailing dogma that we are accidentally chosen physical formations whose strategies were then magically selected to fit.

Additionally, cultures, as far as humans are concerned, are hierarchical in structure. I've mentioned the hierarchy of needs and wondered then about a hierarchy of purposes. I wonder now if there's a hierarchy of trust versus distrust, and while it seems there is, it also seems to be a power hierarchy, where we find the most distrusted up and down the scale. Deception loves hierarchies, it seems, where advantage can be taken at every level.

In a poll I saw concerning trusted professions, they had military officers at the top and car salesmen at the bottom. Lawyers and politicians were also in the bottom half. So far, so good. But then we trust the lawyers and politicians to handle our most telling problems and pay them handsomely for those services in the bargain.

So in effect we may not trust them to be honest, but trust them with top positions in a socially responsible hierarchy. In short, we trust them for their abilities to lie on our behalves. With lawyers, we trust as well that they will keep our secrets and they generally do. Unless our enemies are their clients and then their lying, as far as we're concerned, will have no mercy.

Politicians could be worse than the above, especially since more of them than not are also lawyers. We know, at least unconsciously, when they're lying as well. But if it's for our mutual purposes, to defeat the politician we don't like for whatever reasons, we approve of the lying. Not knowing that in our hopeful acceptance of their lies as more true than absolutely false, we've also helped our politicians to deceive us further.

But in the end what we've seemingly evolved is a hierarchy of personal strategies. Each of us born with the ability to use all of these strategies, but with some much more trusted by our subconscious selves than others. I could speculate that these differences were in part the instinctive products of our much earlier diversity of cultures, but at this point in my research that's just a guess. Another one that someone else might choose to run with, I can hope.

Personal strategies are ordinarily referred to as personalities. To learn more about that subject, you might start with the Wikipedia entry under Facet, and then go to the Five Factor Model section. They show trust as a factor of agreeableness and then show emotionally stable people as trustworthy, The inference is that the less agreeable and less stable will have less trust and be less trustworthy. Nothing there about the most clever being at times the most deceptive, or all of us using deception as an asset to any of these personality facets.

Cheating? Supposedly to act dishonestly or unfairly in order to gain an advantage. If so, why don't the various studies of microbial and animal behaviors just call these "cheating" acts deceptive and get on with it?

Possibly because we don't know that much about the effects of deceptive strategies on our own behaviors, and that in turn because we've been told very little about the use of deception by the tiny creatures that make up 90% of our "human" cells. And again I'm referring to the vast variety of species of bacteria and other microbes that are distributed somewhat randomly and unequally among all of us.

Because, as I noted above, most of the scientific papers I've read about bacteria and their essentially cooperative natures, say next to nothing about deception, but a lot about the bacteria and others like them who occasionally "cheat". They are not seen as deceivers, apparently, as the cheating is supposedly an openly observable affair.

But even when you might suspect some bacteria are keeping secrets from each other, they apparently aren't seen as doing so with deceptive intent. Yet it's clear that bacteria use deceptive tactics against competing strains of their own species, and certainly there are dangerous strains of bacteria who work to deceive our immune systems regularly. And their quorum sensing strategies are certainly planned to effectively sneak up on their prey.

And further, there's much talk about "cheater" resistance developing in bacteria, amoeba, and other forms of microorganisms, and opposition to that resistance must then develop as well. And if deception isn't used as a tactic by all sides at this point, then what is? Except that again, the papers I've seen on these behaviors don't refer to deception as necessary to any of these opposing strategies, and even refer to similar behaviors in animals (that to me are clearly deceptive) as merely 'cheating' consistent with the bacterial or amoebic ways of doing those same things.

But again, if cheating is defined as acting "dishonestly or unfairly in order to gain an advantage" and dishonesty is a form of deception, what's my problem? Well, possibly it's that deception is not necessarily dishonest. Nor is it necessarily unfair. Nor is it necessarily immoral, as cheating would most likely be when applied to humans.

I'm reminded of another way that behavioral scientists seem to misuse their terms in dealing with other forms of life than ours, which involves their use of "altruism" to describe cooperative traits in these other creatures, and seen specifically in zoology as "behavior of an animal that benefits another at its own expense." On the premise, presumably, that when such behaviors are engaged in by humans, they are seen by us as requiring unreasonable sacrifices. Therefor, if done by other forms of life on earth, these actions will supposedly require similar forms of sacrifice, which has seemed to make altruism in general quite hard to explain as an evolutionary benefit to any species.

I'd argue that these actions are quite reasonable from an evolutionary standpoint, and I'll have more to say about that later. I mention it now as being somewhat analogous to other ways we sometimes get things backwards when comparing our behaviors to those of our predecessors in the evolutionary chain. But in my view, the motives that continue to propel us won't have changed. The strategies and their growing complexity most certainly will have.

Scot Atran, the noted Anthropologist and Psychologist, wrote a paper titled "A Cheater–Detection Module?" A module being one of those same yet different things evolutionary psychologists have used to replace Dawkins' failed concept of memes as an evolutionary conveyor of traits. But Scot didn't find modules all that viable as evolutionary processors either. (Nor do I.) So far so good, except that paper mentioned "cheater" 38 times, "deceit" once, and "deception" never.

It so happens that in this paper Scot sees cheating as a defection from cooperation, or from "reciprocal altruism" as he and others called it, Using vampire bat groups as an example, he writes:

"To survive, vampire bats foray each night in search of a blood meal. Chances of success are highly variable and a bat will die if unfed for sixty hours. To reduce this variance and prevent starvation, bats with blood-filled stomachs will regurgitate some of this valuable and hard- to-get resource to other hungry bats. The best predictor of whether or not a bat will share with a needy nonrelative is whether or not the nonrelative has previously shared food. Vampire bats may be able to recognize cheaters during grooming, when they can best perceive whose stomachs are most distended with food and yet are not sharing. It is unclear, however, whether a bat that fails to regurgitate is recognized as a 'cheater' only by individuals the bat has

denied, or acquires a 'reputation' as a defector when other 'cooperators' observe the bat's denial to those in need. It is also unclear whether cooperation is a quid pro quo or "from each according to its ability", whether cheaters recognize the consequences of their 'defection', and whether cheaters or would-be cheaters learn from the 'punishments' meted out."

I won't quote from the rest of this paper as you can easily find it online and download it. My quarrel is basically with the paragraph above. Because it's obvious that the cheaters here are not doing their cheating business openly, and have clearly used more complicated strategies than simple cheating would require They weren't simply selfish and indifferent to the rules by which their group cooperated. These particular bats were motivated to intentionally deceive.

There's no reference in this paper to a possible violation of another's trust, and these animals may not seem intelligent enough to engage in what would truly be intentional deception. But deceptive strategies that have become inherent to a species over time have intention as what I'd call a prior option. If they've made an assessment of the probable success of acting on that strategy, then there's little need for second guessing involved.

And obviously these bats are not created equally, as otherwise there'd be no such thing as cheating either. All, by that equality theory, being uniformly good at following their rules. Which has never been the case in any of our necessarily hierarchical societies. Experiences at every level, if only due to times and places, are necessarily different for every known individual in every species. And different strategic options have evolved for each change to be expected in their opportunities.

Anticipation of change is the key here, or what I'd call an evolutionary purpose server, and another thing that waits to be discussed. So while it may have seemed at the time that these bats weren't intelligent enough to engage in the sort of deception I've described, all species are turning out in closer examination these days to be a lot more intelligent than we've thought. Again, because intelligence is inherent to the increasingly complex ways we've learned to use our long instinctive strategies.

Deception also has that moral connotation that cheating somehow doesn't. To the extent that the actions of these bats were hidden and therefor, to humans, would be morally suspect, the lack of any moral rules that apply to bats may be one reason why cheating seemed more applicable to these bat behaviors than the relative dishonesty of deception.

But the fact is that deception is a natural behavior for all animals (humans included) when the necessity to deceive has been presented to them. In my opinion, all morality comes down to what we can be trusted by our cultures to do right, and distrusted if we do it wrong. And in that sense all beings with a culture have moral rules and standards to adhere to. So bats and bacteria can in their own ways be immoral, and therefor as deceptive in those ways as all the rest of us.

From a note to a friend some time ago:
"Bacteria, fungi, insects, plants, animals all use some form of trickery, and all devise some form of combatting trickery.
Biologists call it cheating, but they are wrong, because when trickery is one of the rules of life, it's not cheating.
Only humans call it cheating because we think the rules we made up for each other are also nature's rules.
But nature's rules are to do what works as long as it keeps working.
There's no evil in nature. We invented the concept to counterbalance our own predatory instincts. We are the only species that can fight each other through communication of abstract concepts. So we fashion those concepts to trick both our friends and enemies without really knowing where those underlying strategies came from.
We fashion our various gods to control what we have fashioned our various devils to perform. We use them as pawns in a complicated game of trust or distrust. We are like ghosts of Hamlet crying out, "To trust or not to trust, that is the question!!""

Ok, so it's corny. But I still kind of like it.

Altruism. Let's have another whack at that.
From my dictionary:
altruism ˈaltro͞oˌizəm|

noun
the belief in or practice of disinterested and selfless concern for the well-being of others : some may choose to work with vulnerable elderly people out of altruism.
• Zoology behavior of an animal that benefits another at its own expense.

From Wikipedia, also in reference to altruism:
"D.S. Wilson and his co-author E.O. Wilson (no relation) have become well known for the quote, "Selfishness beats altruism within groups. Altruistic groups beat selfish groups. Everything else is commentary." This quote appeared in their paper, "Rethinking the Theoretical Foundation of Sociobiology."

Yes, I set up that reference on purpose as I had written to D.S. Wilson often on issues that included this subject. And he had also written, according to my notes, that cultures allow group selection because they also enable a vital biological asset: altruism.

And let me say right here that I haven't been selecting either of these Wilsons as easy pickins'. They are two of the best evolutionary biologists out there. If I hadn't selected them as the best people to make this particular argument with, I'd have less reason to trust that my differences with theirs made any difference to anyone else.

D.S. Wilson once had a blog at Huffington Post, and I wrote this to him:
*"05/16/2009
And did you ever consider that if selfishness beats altruism within groups, it's when the goal is not to achieve success as a group but to achieve success as an individual within the group - the purpose of the group formation itself being more or less incidental to the purposes of these individuals.
But when groups themselves compete, and the altruistic appear to beat the selfish, what you seemingly designate as an altruistic group is in actuality a group of individuals acting altruistically among themselves to create a group that will be, in effect, the more competitive. Making it therefor more selfish than the competing group of strategically selfish individuals, who by failing to cooperate for a common goal, lose as a group.*

And thus if you create groups that can work toward a goal as one individual, you have much the same dynamic in group competition as you do in individual competition. When the goal is selfish, the selfish always win. Paradox dissolved."

He didn't answer me on that one. Possibly because if I'm attempting to explain these things to others, I should first explain them better to myself. (Also because I made some serious mistakes in other comments which I won't reiterate.)

Also the experimental models from that paper, "Rethinking the Theoretical Foundation of Sociobiology." (and from others) show that the selection is being influenced by the groups, but the mechanisms can't be specifically determined by the models; and apparently don't have to be, any more than "natural selection" theories in general specify the wheres and whats of mechanisms involved in their processes. They just tell us that we (as life forms) don't operate the central evolutionary mechanism, and that instead it operates us. As these group selection processes of the Wilsons are also said to do.

So let me propose a thought version of what these models would purportedly demonstrate. Consider these selfish and altruistic groups as competing football teams. Let's say both groups are to have 24 men ready to play on the field, and 16 or so in reserve. Assuming that from the general population, you could round up a group of inherently selfish men, and forgetting that all social groups will tend to be hierarchical in other ways, how did that "selfish" group choose who were most likely to make the team and play the game, as opposed to those most likely not to? Obviously (in my thoughts that is) they competed among themselves for the spots on the playing team, with the losers to sit the game out on the bench. And the competition was as aggressive as each man could make it, no holds barred that they could get away with. (If you think this kind of thing won't happen in reality, check out the effects of "stack ranking" on employees.)

Naturally, the rules that the selfish made for this internal competition were not the same as those for playing in the actual game. At that time they were to work hard together as a team, but in the practice they were to work as hard or harder against each other to get on the team at all. Every man worked for himself unless he could get another man to work for him as well. (Hey, they can't all be selfish, can they?) But even then, cooperation was just a fluke to defeat the fellow selfish, right?. In the end, they'd defeat each other in practice any "legal" physical and tactical way they could. And the team that went on the field to play those altruistic fools knew they were made up of the toughest in the bunch. And they were right.

In the meanwhile, the group of inherently altruistic players (I can't imagine where they got them either) practiced just as hard, but with a different strategy. Each man agreed to give all others as much playing time in practice as possible. Each tried hard to work on improving what they perceived as the other's weaknesses. If the other guy was made the better player on the bargain, all the better in their minds for the team.

And they were also right. When playing in the actual game, the (mostly) altruistic men, by having helped each other to survive, may or may not have been as capable physically as the (mostly) selfish men who'd learned to beat each other for the same survival purposes. But the difference was the altruistic men were constantly reminded they were cooperating for a selfish goal. The selfish men of course took that goal for granted, but unfortunately in concentrating on their selfish strategies, they were unable to make an equally cooperative effort to attain it. (Or so I thought.)

Few players of the actual game of football are good enough or dumb enough to be as selfish as portrayed in this thought exercise. And few coaches. But what I've tried to do here is flesh out the proposed scenarios that would make the end games either work or not work. I haven't said that much about the "whys' of the matter, or when these systems 'might or mightn't" work, but then neither have the Wilsons.
They (and others like them) realize that these types of models don't determine "whys," and don't see why they should. But if they did, the Wilsons might have discovered, as you may have, why they've got the motivational factors somewhat backwards.

In reality, groups made up of cooperative people beat the groups made up of selfish people all the time. But not because the cooperative people are intrinsically or inherently unselfish. It's because their short and long term interests can't always be the same. "Within group" cooperation is always in the strategic short term interests of any group, whether or not its plans or purposes or goals for its longer term relations with outsider groups might require it to be either friendly (cooperative) or unfriendly (selfish).

(Wilson once conceded that these experimental models, which essentially relied on mathematical comparisons, were not perfect, precisely because the hypothetical assumptions they were required to examine were not perfect. What our animals and such are observed to do is one thing, but the reasons that they do it are another thing. I don't have any notes confirming this exchange of views however.)

But the main problem I have with the Wilsons, for going to all this trouble to try to demonstrate and prove these differences, is that such groups of predominately selfish people hardly ever exist successfully in nature. Groups are held together by mutual trust, not mutual distrust. And groups relate to other groups as "friendly"" due to trust, and "selfish" due to distrust.

Which reminds me to point out that these experimental models are also set up like games, where each side may be friendly and trustworthy off the field but are forced to be unfriendly and distrustful on the field. And we seem to think there must be winners and losers in every thing that fits the definition of a game. And thus the game of war becomes the most seriously distrustful that we play.

The game of life however was evolved with different rules. If we really understood its strategic processes, we might find a game where winners must *outnumber* losers. Model that one if you can.

Speaking of more ways to win than lose, note this I wrote to Wilson earlier:
"05/13/2009
You make the mistake of assuming altruism and selfishness are separate genetically based traits. They are not. If anything, they are optional choices in a spectrum of strategic responses regulated by a combination of genetic drivers.
Everyone has access to them by individually different measure, just as we differ individually in personalities. You can assign students roles to play in

games, but the fact that the results will be then predictable tells us
something about the effectiveness of the strategies, but nothing much
about how the actual differences in individual personalties molds these
strategies in "real consequence" circumstances. And nothing much about
the entire range of strategies that make up the reciprocity tool kit."

No response to that either, but what I failed to do was bring up the
causative effects of trust. Yes, trust has causative effects. (Otherwise I
shouldn't call it functional, should I.) Social groups don't work without a set
of rules that the members can be trusted (more or less) to follow. Which
would be why, as I had also written without grasping its full meaning, *"the*
structural group that can work toward a goal with the minimum of defectors
or cheaters has been designated in the literature as a cooperative
hierarchy." (Yes, I used the words defectors and cheaters just as the
people I'm criticizing now for doing that had done. My bad.)

But I should have added that reciprocity depends on each party's trust that
agreements to reciprocate will stand.
And agreements to reciprocate are what altruism (also functional) is all
about.
One definition of trust for example is: *"the state of being responsible for*
someone or something."
One definition of altruism: *"the belief in or practice of disinterested and*
selfless concern for the well-being of others."
One definition of reciprocate: *"respond to (a gesture or action) by making a*
corresponding one."

Three sides of the same strategic coin, perhaps. There's a fourth side to
that coin, however, and that's distrust. And if I haven't said it this way
earlier, I should have: All strategies of living beings have evolved to serve
a strategic purpose. And the strategy of reciprocation is a bonding strategy
that holds all social groups together. There are no cultures that are without
their rules for reciprocation. All members of these cultural groups will trust
each other to heed those rules. And all members will recognize in one way
or another that what we call "altruism" is the trust that all will carry out their
respective duties to protect each other from whatever distrustful forces of
our natures attempt to sever their strategic bonds and divert their purposes.

These are not concepts that the earlier evolving groups and their members have had to consciously think about at all. The rules have been taught by intelligent examples of what to trust, and enforced by intelligent examples of what happens to distrusters (better known as those cheaters and defectors that we came across here earlier).

Speaking of what happens to the less altruistic distrusters, I turn again to David Sloan Wilson and Edward O. Wilson. In the American Science article, Evolution for the Good of the Group (the process known as group selection), they noted that human hunter gatherer societies differed from the supposed "cheater" advantage dynamic in other biological groupings in that they were fiercely egalitarian (meaning they operated with a very high degree of altruism). They proposed this altruism was due to selection for teamwork which acted to suppress cheating activities.

Before I comment on that proposal further, I must point out that there's much more to this paper than discussing cheating, and it's very difficult to follow for the average person - which when it comes to interpreting the jargon of the multilevel selection crowd, includes me. And then there is a large crowd of equally proficient jargonists, who don't believe in group selection at all. One being Steven Pinker, Professor of Psychology; Harvard University. Who I'll have a few bones to pick with later, as he's far on the other side of all of us here, when it comes to the evolution of traits.

But what this Wilsons paper also shows is the extent to which the advocates of their theoretical hypotheses will go to demonstrate the accuracy of their premises. Their methods of testing, they say, including social psychological experimentation and multilevel modeling equations. Using premises, however, that if approached from a different analytical angle, turn out to be, at least from that new angle, wrong.

That newer angle being to come at the matter by divining a behavior's purpose on the assumption that all behaviors were based on the evolutionary history of experiencing the expected and anticipated results, and not on some rather nebulous speculations as to that behavior's genetic fitness. But fitness is the Wilsons' angle.

In biology, Darwinian fitness or simply fitness of a biological trait describes how successful an organism has been at passing on its genes. The more likely that an individual is able to survive and live longer to reproduce, the higher is the fitness of that individual. (There are also two ways through which fitness can be measured, absolute fitness, and relative fitness. Feel free to look into that if you're interested.)

But we're concerned here, regardless of fitness, as to how cheating and altruism, the putative genetic traits in focus, achieved the status of being genetically separate. As well as appearing to serve purposes that are more antagonistic than complimentary to each other. And the question from my angle is, have these traits evolved to contend with different circumstances, or were they naturally selected, as the Wilson's might have it, so that circumstances have had to contend with them?

So in addition to proposing that the fierce egalitarianism of the human hunter gatherer groups was due to selection for teamwork, which then acted to suppress cheating activities, what else of interest here did the Wilsons' paper say about cheating and its alter ego, altruism?

Well, what it basically says about altruism is that the level of selection for the trait is in the group rather than in the individual. Nothing said about the contention of others that it's the experience of adapting to the group that causes the individual to adapt its behavioral traits accordingly. (In addition there are references to breeding the individual for the trait, not wondering how the trait existed to be bred for to begin with.)

They also wrote: *"For example, animals might cooperate because they have genes in common ("kin selection") or because of the likelihood of reciprocal aid in the future. In this way, apparent altruism was interpreted as enlightened self-interest. It became almost mandatory for authors to assure their readers that group selection was not being invoked."*

But that group selection comment was simply a red herring. If cooperation requires mutual trust, then altruism comes naturally from that as a mutually trusting strategy. It doesn't matter whether the individuals are in the same group or not, as long as the groups are in the same culture. Or the people simply from two cultures that value the efficacy of mutual trust in equal measure. And all of us know from experience that there's a reliable truth to this trust dynamic. We don't need the sort of mathematical modeling that tells us mutual trust is somehow a reliable illusion.

The other comments about altruism are largely in the same vein, that altruism is selectively disadvantageous within groups and evolves in the total population only by "between group" selection. But here's a thought: take altruism out of a group and see what happens. I expect the group will fall apart. Take cheating out and see what happens. Christ only knows where that group went to.

Of course we must leave cheating in the mix if it has co-evolved with altruism. Although the Wilsons have written otherwise:
"These interacting layers of competition and evolution are like Russian matryoshka dolls nested one within another. At each level in the hierarchy natural selection favors a different set of adaptations. Selection between individuals within groups favors cheating behaviors, even at the expense of the group as a whole. Selection between groups within the total population favors behaviors that increase the relative fitness of the whole group— although these behaviors, too, can have negative effects at a still-larger scale.

They also wrote:
"Prudently managing a shared resource benefits all members of a group, including any "cheaters" who consume more than their share. Genes associated with cheating would therefore spread through the group, and the propensity for cooperative resource management would be undermined."

The rest of what was written on cheaters was in my opinion even more misguided. That is, if you accept with me that so called cheating, along with altruism, are survival strategies, and are derived from the original trusting and deceiving strategies that have fueled the evolutionary processes of life. (Again, assuming I and some others are at all correct about our being in an experience driven system.)

And to address the initial proposition that the fiercely altruistic egalitarianism of hunter gatherer societies was due to selection for teamwork which acted to suppress cheating activities, I have to say the Wilsons may have wasted a lot of time with that one.

Because if cheating is the result of being genetically selfish rather than genetically altruistic, and selfishness in a cooperative group is being equated to cheating, the sanctions applied to cheaters can only temporarily suppress the behavior - and, if cooperation is in a large sense genetically altruistic, suppression of genetic cheaters won't convert them to the practice of genetic altruism. Not the way to make a true cooperator in other words. So if the Wilsons were to be correct on the one hand, what they'll have on the other hand is teamwork between a lot of suppressed cheaters and another lot of unsuppressed altruists. Hardly a fiercely dedicated group.

Which encourages me to digress a bit below:

What the Wilsons (and others like them) do not mention was that the hunter gatherers were cooperating to compete for their world's natural resources. And as it turns out, the competing forms of life almost inevitably have become their own best resource. We have discovered that the best way, and perhaps the only way, to survive on earth is, of course, to eat each other.

We take this for granted as the most natural of all our survival processes, but we don't seem to realize that all of our evolutionary processes depend on recognizing that if we did NOT eat our related living forms we would NOT survive. We have no choice to NOT eat what some of us would call our other selves.

Well, you say, it's for that reason that a lot of us will only eat plants. But plants are life forms as well, and some of them survive precisely because we eat them. And the same goes for both wild and domesticated animals. So if you thought I was implying that eating our "life-selves" is a bad thing, I wasn't. It's neither good nor bad by nature's principles, it simply is. But this natural practice is the source of all our conflicts, and the generating force of all our living strategies.

Yes, I think that force is the right word to use here. A situation that compels us to react intelligently is a force. And especially if it has compelled us to evolve.

Eating and producing life to be eaten is an intelligently acquired process that life could not have accidentally fallen into, or fallen even more intelligently into carrying out the entire operation up to now.

Cooperating to compete. But don't we also compete to cooperate? Sure, but when it comes to competing for resources, that competition is the impetus that makes cooperation happen at all. We can, in other words, cooperate to compete for resources. We cannot compete to cooperate for resources. There's no strategic purpose there at all.

So as I said at the beginning, it's my position that all evolution is the proximate result of the entity involved reacting strategically to its experience. And I'd be at least subconsciously inclined to favor any thought experiments that supported that position. And those who don't support it would hardly be convinced, by these less than scientific efforts, that they're wrong. But luckily I've found more to offer than my own attempts at experimental reasoning here.

I came upon a recent article at the Edge website that tends to bring some focus to the evolutionary theories "competing" to apply to what is ultimately our "group or no group" selection problem. (Hey, taking advantage of luck is what we do.) It's called The False Allure of Group Selection, an original essay from the well known Steven Pinker, Professor of Psychology; Harvard University, and with E. O. Wilson is his particular target. Other than having that target in common, I disagree with Pinker in almost every aspect of his thesis. For him, the direct effects of experience on change would appear to have no bearing on the progression of our evolutionary changes at all.

But I'll limit my comments to the questions at hand concerning how our behavioral traits have more likely evolved from our most basic strategies. And how Pinker and Wilson represent the theories that have been off the mark there for too long a time. (And readers should feel free to read the complete essay to determine if I'm cherry picking for the easy targets. Which of course I am.)

Let's establish first that Pinker has the usual psychological explanations of how altruism is supposed to work, and has this to say: *"The huge literature on the evolution of cooperation in humans has done quite well by applying the two gene-level explanations for altruism from evolutionary biology, nepotism and reciprocity, each with a few twists entailed by the complexity of human cognition."*

OK, gene level explanation, similar to that of the Wilsons though not quite the same. Selfishness also explained as a gene level trait, but what he's really after Wilson for is the idea that these traits could be selected by groups.

Pinker writes, *"I have seen "group selection" used as a loose synonym for the evolution of organisms that live in groups, and for any competition among groups, such as human warfare."*

I say, so what. We need to recognize that all species live to some extent in groups, so one can't really come up with an example of evolution occurring without a group. And yes, without competition, there would have been no need for evolution. (Pinker doesn't think that evolution fulfills a need, of course, since it seems clear he represents the views of neo-Darwinism.)

Pinker says: *"I'll concentrate on the sense of "group selection" as a version of natural selection which acts on groups in the same way that it acts on individual organisms, namely, to maximize their inclusive fitness (alternatively, which acts on groups in the same way it acts on genes, namely to increase the number of copies that appear in the next generation; I will treat these formulations as equivalent)."*

And I say that the only way these assumptions are equivalent is that the formulations would both be wrong. In that natural selection didn't act stochastically, i.e., in a randomly determined way, on groups at all, and was erroneously believed to act that way on genes.

Pinker: "Natural selection is a special explanatory concept in the sciences, worthy, in my view, of Daniel Dennett's designation as "the best idea that anyone ever had." That's because it explains one of the greatest mysteries in science, the illusion of design in the natural world."

I say the greatest mystery to me is why these people persist in arguing that the natural world is bereft of the intelligence to design what clearly took intelligence to build at all.

Pinker: "The core of natural selection is that when replicators arise and make copies of themselves, their numbers will tend, under ideal conditions, to increase exponentially"
"After many generations of replication, the replicators will show the appearance of design for effective replication, while in reality they have just accumulated the copying errors that had successful replication as their effect."

I say, that's just dumb, and Pinker is not dumb. But where he's correct in arguing that group selection, as an explanation for any of our traits, is wrong, his explanation for why we are incapable of designing traits ourselves is dumb. And if It's not exactly Darwinism, it's the Richard Dawkins' version.

From Dawkins' River Out Of Eden, A Darwinian View Of Life, (p.155):
"In a universe of blind forces and physical replication, some people are going to get hurt, others are going to get lucky, and you won't find any rhyme or reason in it, nor any justice. The universe we observe has precisely the properties we should expect if there is, at bottom, no design, no purpose, no evil and no good, nothing but blind, pitiless indifference."

(I lifted that above quote from another good paper to read, Purpose, Meaning & Darwinism, Mary Midgley. Who said, "This is Dawkinsism, not Darwinism.")

Back to Pinker, who followed up with this: "What's satisfying about the theory is that it is so mechanistic. The copying errors (mutations) are random (more accurately, blind to their effects). The outcome of interest is the number of copies in a finite population. The surprising outcome is a *product of the cumulative effects of many generations of replication. If the copying errors were not random (that is, if Lamarck had been correct that changes in an organism arise in response to a felt need, or if creationists were right that a superior intelligence directed mutations to be beneficial to the organism), then natural selection would be otiose—the design could come from the mutation stage."*

I say to that, exactly! This Dawkinsistic stuff IS otiose. The design COULD come from the mutations stage, just as Lamarck, and Baldwin later, have said it does, and many more professional evolutionists say today. They've called this Adaptive Mutation. Google it. Or better, check it out at Wikipedia. (They're also calling this self-engineering, as previously noted.)

Just a bit more from Pinker, and I'll be done with the contretemps with Wilson. I had earlier written some notes on a copy of the Pinker paper, and I'll post them here verbatim starting here with Pinker's writing:

Pinker: "Only when selection operates over multiple generations of replication, yielding a cumulative result that was not obvious from cause and effect applying to a single event, does the concept of natural selection add anything."

Me: Cause and effect applied to adapting to an active and relatively permanent environmental force of change (persistent cold, persistent sun, lack of oxygen, etc.) is the experience that drives us to react intelligently and significantly to that change - until we in fact have adapted to it.

Pinker: "The theory of natural selection applies most readily to genes because they have the right stuff to drive selection, namely making high-fidelity copies of themselves."

Me: Big mistake here, because they aren't high fidelity copies. Identical twins from the same egg aren't exactly identical, but fraternal twins from different sperm, same egg, are never identical.

Pinker: "Granted, it's often convenient to speak about selection at the level of individuals, because it's the fate of individuals (and their kin) in the world of cause and effect which determines the fate of their genes. Nonetheless, it's the genes themselves that are replicated over generations and are thus the targets of selection and the ultimate beneficiaries of adaptations. Sexually reproducing organisms don't literally replicate themselves, because their offspring are not clones but rather composites of themselves and their mates."

Me: Amazing how he doesn't realize that each sperm has a different version of the copied DNA.

Pinker: "Nor can any organism, sexual or asexual, pass onto its offspring the traits it has acquired in its lifetime. Individual bodies are simply not passed down through the generations the way that genes are. As Stephen Jay Gould put it, "You can't take it with you, in this sense above all.""

Me: Is it so hard to understand that genes pass on behavioral strategies and building instructions for their forms? The folding has to be for informational purposes, so why hold that some can come through but not the rest.

And we're done with quoting Pinker for the moment. Although he probably did realize that each sperm has a different version of the copied DNA and his zeal for the emphatic got the better of him. But it seems he meant it when he said that no organism can pass onto its offspring the traits it has acquired in its lifetime. Epigenetics, which according to Wikipedia is "the study of heritable changes in gene expression or cellular phenotype caused by mechanisms other than changes in the underlying DNA sequence," tells us that he's wrong right there. Not one of his best days, apparently.

(I'd put the rest of his published comments and my notes here, but I want to stick to the subject of selfishness and altruism, and where such traits had to come from, so some other time, some other place.)

If anything, this represents some problems that many of the evolutionary true believers are having now. Such as difficulties the Wilsons might have with needing to share some convictions with the Pinker faction in order not to share the others. To believe in group selection, the Wilsons must also be convinced that selfish and altruistic traits are genetically determined and not experientially determined. But the only established theory that supports that is also neo-Darwinism, which Pinker, of that faith as well, now says makes group selection for either selfish or autistic behavior impossible. Which was essentially my argument to start with. Except I don't need to believe in neo-Darwinism at all. Experience making all the difference. Experience that groups have come to trust, that is.

Segueing to speak more broadly about the evolution of our traits, here are excerpts from a paper, The Trouble with Psychological Darwinism, that the philosopher Jerry Fodor wrote in opposition to a Pinker theory of "How the Mind Works." My comments at the time were also in my notes, and I'll put them here as well, verbatim:

Fodor: Many people think that the theory of the selfish gene says that 'animals try to spread their genes'. This misstates . . . the theory. Animals, including most people, know nothing about genetics and care even less. People love their children not because they want to spread their genes (consciously or unconsciously) but because they can't help it. . . What is selfish is not the real motives of the person but the metaphorical motives of the genes that built the person. Genes 'try' to spread themselves (sic) by wiring animals brains so that animals love their kin . . . and then the[y] get out of the way.

My comment: "Genes" 'want' to spread their strategies, and strategies 'want' their forms to survive so that strategies, not just forms, will when necessary evolve. The big question then is, why do strategies care if they evolve or not? And of course they don't 'want' primarily to evolve, they want to continue to exist and in fact have no choice except to want (i.e., anticipate) that. It's apparently impossible for a strategy to not want to be a strategy, since something cannot want successfully to be nothing - nothing's not a foundation for anticipation, wherever that elementary function came from or why it has existed. What was earth life's anticipatory spark, for example, that made it want to choose - when in the past its choices had been 'pre-chosen' (how and why another question) to be activated by the accidents of circumstance?

So there we have it, and if I had it to do over, I wouldn't change a word. Or be able to come up with that particular ideation at all. Was this molecular entity we call life ever a non-chooser to begin with? Or was it a potential chooser without the intelligence to see the need to choose until circumstances would effectively make it have to? Circumstances that somehow made it more intelligent? My answers are that I'm not sure and yes.

It makes sense that the proactive choice making strategies that tend to make the difference between life and non-life have been in existence in the cosmos for a much longer time than such stratagems have taken to become useful to inhabitants of earth. And anyone who will agree that we have a universe with a system of natural laws that operate in a logically predictable fashion, might also agree that the laws that regulate the reactions of all natural substances, in response to contacts with any and all of each other, in that sense are regulating choices. Reactive rather than proactive choices for the most part, but the line between these processes could be more in our imagination than in fact.

And the fact is that life forms make proactive choices that cause things to happen. And these causative strategies would have to have been around before their operational forms developed. And as I wrote in my notes some time ago, *"Strategy is the function of intelligence. The form has no intelligence. It can't choose, even though it's a cause of choice. The function chooses form and/or chooses how it will be caused to adapt."*

That doesn't mean that forms don't offer limits to the nature of any strategies that find them useful. Or that strategies aren't restricted to the limits of our natural geometry, our fractals, our buckyballs, and the like. But there is clearly an intelligent aspect to the versatility and strengths of these archetypical forms, whether the product of some universal trial and error experimentation or not.

And let's get something out of the way before we discuss the nature of our options, without which choice would have no purpose. And that 'something' is the popular conception that the feeling we actually have options which we're free to choose from is an illusion. It's not. Our freedoms are limited by the history of our circumstances, but are not imaginary.

My notes say this: *"We are free to choose because we have to choose. To not choose is to choose not to, even if, as a result, it's to choose to die. To* be deprived of our ability to choose, completely, is our, the chooser's, death in any event. Our purpose, primarily, is to choose. Everything, it seems, in the universe is both required and allowed to choose."

I also wrote: *"We have been "freed" from the necessity to react with a single option that depends largely on circumstances beyond the entity's control, to the having of a choice between reacting to the dictates of the circumstance or of moving proactively to change the circumstance. Thus in that sense all biological .choice making entities have been freed to have the will to choose. We are free to be responsible and thus to take responsibility."*

Also: *"'Free' will is essentially the ability to base decisions on your own predictive selections and assessments as to the best of several options available that you will then be relatively freed from previously directed cause to re-assess and choose from and among. Illusory or not, you will have been caused to be the maker of the choice rather than the conduit of some prior makers choosing."* A little awkward but it makes the point.

I kind of like this one: *"A determinative world is predetermined. An indeterminate one is self (or itself) determined."*
And this: *"If the choice was yours to make, then you are free to make it - it's that simple."* Yes, but don't trust anything completely that starts with if.

Bertrand Russell, On The Notion Of Cause, wrote:
If you already know what the past was, obviously it is useless to wish it different. But also you cannot make the future other than it will be; this again is an application of the law of contradiction.
But you CAN choose to make what "it will be" different from what it would have been if you hadn't chosen to make it other than "it will be" earlier. Choose to chew on that, while everything that changes in the process could in some sense be your chosen fault. Even that which you could not have possibly expected.

What matters in the end is that we are free to react responsively to the unexpected. (Which no doubt reflects the sense from which the word responsible originated.) What also matter are the strategies that our universe may or may not be free to exercise, and as to that, we are at the moment free to speculate.

Getting on with my contention that our evolution depends on the use of intelligent strategies, ours as well as those we are responding to in our environment - the totality of our experiences over time - I'd like to refer you to some writing of Mae-Wan Ho, Geneticist and Biophysicist, excerpted from The End of Bad Science and Beginning Again with Life:

"Finally, the ultimate neo-Darwinian taboo has been broken. Wiesmann's barrier has been breached, and in many different forms, some of which I mentioned already (see box 2).
Box 2
The inheritance of acquired characters
Epigenetic inheritance - inheritance of cellular or gene-expression states such as patterns of DNA methylation, cortical inheritance in ciliates, dauermodifications.
Inheritance of induced changes in genomic DNA - fertilizer treatment of flax and other plants; drug-resistance in mammalian cells insecticide-resistance in insect pests and herbicide-resistance in plants.
Feedback from somatic cells to germ cells - reverse transcription and insertion of cDNA into germ cells, eg. immunoglobulin V genes
'Adaptive' mutations in bacteria, yeast and other cells."

" -- others including myself have written on how those newly discovered processes seriously undermine neo-Darwinian evolutionary theory over 15 years ago10. The evidence against the natural selection of random mutations has grown overwhelming since. Simply stated, organisms can mutate their genes as they are selected; and there is a large degree of non-randomness to mutations.
Recently, molecular geneticist James Shapiro has joined the debate. He is critical of neo-Darwinians like Richard Dawkins and John Maynard Smith who are still clinging to the discredited paradigm. "Localized random mutation, selection operating "one gene at a time" (John Maynard Smith's formulation), and gradual modification of individual functions are unable to provide satisfactory explanation for the molecular data, no matter how much time for change is assumed. There are simply too many potential

degrees of freedom for random variability and too many interconnections to account for."

And yet, the variations are far from random. The processes responsible for the fluidity of the genome form a highly sophisticated regulatory system, which can provide hyper-variability or stability for genes or genomes as required. All organisms, from bacteria to human beings, possess a wide range of repair and proof-reading functions to remove accidental changes to DNA sequences and correct errors resulting from physiological and physical insults. The same cells also possess numerous biochemical mechanisms for changing and reorganizing DNA through 'natural genetic engineering' – processes that include cutting and splicing of DNA molecules into new sequence arrangements (like the immunoglobulin genes). Most frequently, natural genetic engineering involves mobile genetic elements, found in all genomes, which can move from one position to another, enabling organisms to respond to environmental challenges."

Please read that entire paper if you can, But in the meantime, check out this excerpt again from: A 21st Century View of Evolution, James A. Shapiro, James A. Shapiro, Department of Biochemistry and Molecular Biology, University of Chicago, Chicago, IL 60637:

"Molecular genetics has amply confirmed McClintock's discovery that living organisms actively reorganize their genomes. It has also supported her view that the genome can "sense danger" and respond accordingly. The recognition of the fundamentally biological nature of genetic change and of cellular potentials for information processing frees our thinking about evolution. In particular, our conceptual formulations are no longer dependent on the operation of stochastic processes. Thus, we can now envision a role for computational inputs and adaptive feedbacks into the evolution of life as a complex system. Indeed, it is possible that we will eventually see such information-processing capabilities as essential to life itself."

These are just samples of the work and writing being done on what is now referred to as "adaptive mutation." I'll not try to convince you of its accuracy - that's for you to decide by further study. But it "goes a good ways" to back up my contentions that the evolution of life is an intelligent process compelled by the organism's own experience, and not by a series of disinterested accidents that somehow caused a continuum of highly complex changes to our lives and structures, and performed remarkable feats of mimicry as to what looked to the uninitiated like myriads of sets of very well engineered and intelligently organized processes.

But regardless of what we choose to believe about evolution's purposes or lack thereof, all sides seem to agree that life's survival depends on its use of instinctive strategies. You could simply look at trust and distrust as instinctive strategies, if you will, and not concern yourself with where they came from, as long as you can accept the likelihood that they've always been a part of life. Everyone certainly seems to agree that the suspicion of danger has become instinctive, and suspicion is what differentiates trust from distrust and deception, regardless of whether these are 'experience derived' reactions to events or not.

Although if we're not dependent on heritable forms of learned strategies, then those ancient and inert "dead to life" receptacles, where the genetically encoded instinctive action patterns were subsequently stored, would initially have needed to be accidentally and incessantly (if not magically) mutated for an eternity or more to turn that purportedly dead set of molecules into an intelligently directed complex of life.

Note that on what used to be page 74, I wrote: *"And as it turns out, the competing forms of life almost inevitably have become their own best resource. We have discovered that the best way, and perhaps the only way, to survive on earth is of course to eat each other."*
And, *"Eating and producing life to be eaten is an intelligently acquired process that life could not have accidentally fallen into, or fallen even more intelligently into carrying out the entire operation up to now."*

The above shows us a great and timeless worldwide evolution of highly complex living strategies. Nothing in our science or philosophy can adequately explain how this conglomeration came to be, other than by the intelligently orchestrated evolution of itself.

So on the assumption that life wasn't also required to invent strategic processes to enable it to further invent what was already itself, we have to wonder where these complexingly intelligent procedures came from, if not from the universe around us that the energy and matter we evolved from had quite obviously come from earlier.

And as I wrote on formerly page 81, *"It makes sense that the proactive choice making strategies that tend to make the difference between life and non-life have been in existence in the cosmos for a much longer time than such stratagems have taken to become useful to the inhabitants of earth."*

And while it's not my intention here to discuss the effects of the various religions on our cultures and the oddities of those policies and plans they've offered us, I have to add this: In case you're inclined to think that a God or two invented all our strategies, and so "case closed," I suspect that it's our acquired strategies that invented any of the Gods we've seen around us first. Even so, it doesn't mean that your particular shibboleths are unsuitable, just that authoritative sources claiming the right to pronounce them holy might be suspect.

The authoritative voice that I'd prefer to turn to for advice about the universe's choices would be that of the recently deceased theoretical physicist, John Archibald Wheeler. He wanted to understand the whys of the universe, as much as to know the whats, whens, wheres and hows. (And unlike some of his fellows, he could recognize the unanswerable from the answerable, but that's a story for another time.)

Regarding my statement earlier that choices made by non-living entities in the universe were "reactive rather than proactive for the most part," both the reactive and proactive parts would be included in what Wheeler would refer to as "binary choice."

And with Wikipedia as my source, I'm informed as follows:
"In 1990, Wheeler suggested that information is fundamental to the physics of the universe. According to this "it from bit" doctrine, all things physical are information-theoretic in origin.
Wheeler: It from bit. Otherwise put, every "it" — every particle, every field of force, even the space-time continuum itself — derives its function, its

meaning, its very existence entirely — even if in some contexts indirectly — from the apparatus-elicited answers to yes-or-no questions, binary choices, bits. "It from bit" symbolizes the idea that every item of the physical world has at bottom — a very deep bottom, in most instances — an immaterial source and explanation; that which we call reality arises in the last analysis from the posing of yes — no questions and the registering of equipment-evoked responses; in short, that all things physical are information-theoretic in origin and that this is a participatory universe."

I don't necessarily agree with everything else he might have said, but that was a winner. And of course he's not the only one who's said that, but he said it well.

I'm also aware that those such as Buckminster Fuller believed that the universe, like the life it has allowed to exist on earth, operates with an anticipatory system. He reportedly said, "Experience had clearly demonstrated an a priori anticipatory and only intellectually apprehendable orderliness of interactive principles operating in the universe into which we are born." Unfortunately for my purposes here, Buckminster also saw this as evidence of the existence of a God.

But another question that Wheeler and others had somewhat famously asked was, "Why is there something rather than nothing?" The only feasible answer being that there must always have been something, since logic, by the same token that allows for the possibility of Gods, would not allow the possibly of the nothing that these Gods had supposedly overcome. The universal systems thus needing to have evolved themselves from something that could not conceivably have created itself.

From my notes: *"Muse 4-9-11: A universal law is not a law so much as a description of the qualities of its forces and its related matter that the universe has developed over time to reach stability, and that we have then discovered to be what we see as a law. Because it seems (illusively) that these are regulations that the universe must follow, not understanding perhaps that the universe hasn't so much followed as has created them,"*

And I don't know anything more about that now than I did then. Or know that something had to come from anything other than itself to be here. Or that an evolving intelligence had to come from anything that could not intelligently evolve.

On formerly page 4 of this book, I wrote the following: *"In any case, honesty and deception are not necessarily antithetical - which I've tried to explain in another essay that I wrote to help out a former client - not expecting at the time to write a book about it. (So look for this essay at the end of this book.)"*

So here's that essay, warts and all, offered hopefully as a fitting way to end this volume. I won't identify the client, but I owe that person a lot for inspiring me to get off the dime and actually do what up to then had been an empty promise to myself to someday do it.

A Brief Essay on Trust

O wad some Power the giftie gie us
To see oursels as ithers see us!

The above is of course from a poem by Robert Burns. It echoes in a way what we all may have wished from time to time. But would such knowledge be a gift without reservation? In my view, it would be good to know with more accuracy how others perceive us, but only if we don't then measure ourselves by that and that alone. Others, as we're often painfully aware, may project their opinions of us basically to control or manipulate us - to attract us, dominate us, persuade us, etc. That's fine to the extent that we realize where we need to be controlled, or influenced, but not so fine if we try to change our behavior simply to fit someone else's view of what we ought to do, or how we ought to be.

We should instead use such knowledge to learn who among these others we can trust, and learn how to gain the trust of those deserving individuals in return. We need this knowledge to know what we can expect from these others, as expectations are, in effect, what we "trust" will occur in the future. In the sense that plans, predictions, and expectations all depend on learning who and what to trust, an understanding of the nature and importance of trust in human affairs has to be essential, in my opinion, to any understanding of life itself.

Perhaps the first step in this learning process is to recognize that trustworthiness is not a quality that goes hand in hand with honesty. The concepts are not interchangeable, and the former is more important in any society than the latter, even though we all give the most emphasis to the latter in our various sermonizing, and in our fables, myths, commandments, codes of ethics, etc. We profess to measure trust by honesty, and honesty by someone's perceived truthfulness, yet we all recognize unconsciously that some people who never lie cannot always be trusted, and that some who we trust the most are those who we know will lie on occasion.

So the point I'm trying to make is that perceptions that rely on honesty can be wrong, and to assume you can trust an honest man is to assume first that he really is honest, and second, that honesty equates to trustworthiness even if your first assumptions are correct.

Why then shouldn't one assume honesty pretty much denotes trustworthiness? Because there are other components of being trustworthy that are equally as important. Take judgement, for example. Would you follow an honest man who you know to also be an idiot? The answer is obvious. Would you follow a liar who only lies about his past, but can lead you safely through danger, or solve the hardest of puzzles? The answer is not quite as obvious, but when you look at trust as situational, which it most often is, then the answer will likely be yes.

I used honesty as the first example of the many things people look for in deciding who to trust or not trust because it is the primary indicator in most cultures. But trust is such a complicated subject that to this day I don't think it has been adequately explored or its importance fully understood. Trust is engendered in part by how people look, for another example. It's in the genes, so to speak. The people perceived as better looking are trusted more because others are getting a message that they will produce better children, as well as be expected (i.e. trusted) to rise higher in society, fight better, hunt better, and so forth. Add height to that, and if the good looking person is also tall, there is even more trust involved in certain situations.

But of course one can also be too tall to trust with some tasks, and too good looking to be trusted by those who are wary of the proverbial traveling salesman.

More examples could be cited, but the upshot is that we can get a lot of mixed signals which make deciding who to trust in general, as well as in particular, quite difficult. Getting someone to like you, for example, often involves getting them to trust you at the same time (and vice versa). But you may also find you can trust someone (a competent professional, for example) that you don't particularly like because he wears a wig, or spits when he talks. Okay, he won't likely sire a prize child, but you can still have reason to trust him to cure your ulcers, or fix your roof.

And the mention of mixed signals brings us to another, and very important, aspect of assessing trust, which involves the broad area of deception, and the role it plays in human affairs (and in all animal affairs as well). Deception, by definition, is providing intentionally misleading information to others. But the aim and purpose of deception is always to violate trust by sending false signals that mimic some aspect of trustworthiness.

Generally speaking, the trustworthiness involved is either an inherent quality of something you are mimicking (a wolf wearing sheep's clothing), or a quality in the victim that can be induced to accept a false signal (the wolf can also make a noise that sounds to our ears like a sheep). Of course if you have never believed that sheep are inherently harmless, and thus don't trust them to begin with, the deception in these instances won't succeed, no matter how well you emulate a sheep.

But this brings us (or me) to an important element of what trust means, because it has to be defined in part by how it functions. It's most important function, in my view, is to act as a bridge across uncertainty, because there is almost nothing a person can be 100% certain about from birth to death. Every action a person (or any animal) takes is in some way a leap of faith. The mind, consciously or unconsciously, human brain or lizard brain, makes decisions based on limited knowledge, assesses probable consequences, either as governed by instinct as to what has allowed the species to survive up to now, or as governed by more abstract *assessments made by one's (so-called) rational mind, but again with the emotional signals from the instinctive area of our brains prodding our judgement.*

In short, life could not have developed without organisms finding a way to take the first step into the unknown where danger dictated that that step would very likely be fatal. The way, if I interpret Darwin correctly, was to take multiple steps and "learn" what worked and didn't work by trial and error. There was arguably no thought process involved in this at the beginning, and it's my guess that the mechanism of trust became a factor only when rudimentary brains developed that could make calculations.

Of course there was no word for this mechanism at the outset, but it was essentially the process developed to assess probabilities of success based on alternative paths of action that the situation at hand seemed to present, whatever need or hunger was the motivating force. The more advanced organisms, In choosing which path to then take, took that which was least uncertain (or most certain if you will). And that action in the face of uncertainty, when experienced by those of us who developed a language with which to express symbols and abstract ideas, was referred to as the process of "trust" (or the equivalent guttural utterance).

So again in my view, brains, and those of humans in particular, developed as devices to solve the problem most essential to survival: that of learning which objects, desires, or goals to trust, and not to trust. And every step taken in fulfilling these needs and desires also included, or came to include, determining how to defeat deception, or counter with deception, when to offer trust in return for trust, or when to meet trust with deception, and eventually how and when to form bonds that relied on mutuality of trust.

And thus (again in my less than humble opinion) the results of everything we do are dependent on how well we decide at every step what avenues can or cannot be trusted.

While we already do all of this unconsciously (to use the term loosely), we really don't consider that this mechanism is the basis of what we are doing. We rationalize our actions after the fact, and attribute our successes to other factors, when those factors may or may not have had anything to do with the outcome. Similarly, we justify or otherwise explain our mistakes by laying the blame where it doesn't belong, especially when it's in someone else's interest to persuade us to do so.

This is perhaps a good place to pause, and to point out that what I have said about trust is not necessarily original, and certainly far from complete - although it's something I have been mulling over for a long time. And I haven't used any quotes or done any research while writing this, so it's basically just my opinion, and I can't give any assurance as to what part of what I've said is accurate, assuming any of it is.

But maybe I've presented some ideas as to a fresh way to look at things, and to examine others, and their motives, and to examine and measure our own opinions and motives. And hopefully I have offered some direction for deciding on the better path or paths to take when faced with some future dilemma.

The floor is now open for questions and discussion of the printed material.

Addendum 1

Think about this as well, which in fact is something I have pondered upon (is that a proper phrase?) for years , and which may have been the genesis of my larger theorizing on trust:

In every society, there are acceptable lies (flattery, blarney, puffery) that almost everybody learns to tell, and in a way, those who DON'T tell those lies are not to be trusted, because they are, in effect, violating the rules under which trust is granted. If they don't follow those particular customs, people will then ask, how can they be expected to follow other such arbitrary rules in that culture?

The lies told that are NOT thus sanctioned are those we would call material falsehoods, lies that are used for deliberate deception, and that could have consequences adverse to the person who believed they were true statements. The "acceptable" lies on the other hand are not seen as material because nobody in the culture really relies on them as guides to future behavior. They may believe them as possibly being true, but not with any degree of certainty. So people will still trust those who tell these "white lies," providing this behavior isn't carried to extremes. The line to be crossed here differs from culture to culture.

In the Western world, however, we have long crossed over that line, and are inundated with such lies in advertising, politics, law, and business in general. We have essentially had to come up with a new category to delineate the otherwise gray area between white lies and black ones, and have begun to call this area officially as "bullshit" (a term heretofore reserved as an informal and symbolic depiction of certain types of deception).

But what also appears to be common to all cultures is that we trust those who tell white lies more than the rest because they are seen essentially as trying to avoid doing us harm, and because we have come to expect and trust those close to us to use such means to protect our egos and illusions.

How the need for these illusions fits into the overall picture of "trust" would be food for another long (and possibly irrelevant) essay. But it has a lot to do with the necessity sometimes for self-deception. The mechanisms in our brains that warn us to distrust and shy away from danger seem also to induce us to shy away from what we might call the "awful truths." We distrust our own conclusions if they are something we are afraid to hear, and for which some plausible substitute "truth" can be found. In effect, we substitute hope for uncertainty if nothing else allows us to proceed with any confidence. Hope then becomes part of the stuff myths are made of, and myths by circumstance are necessarily different for each culture, and in essence define and have given rise to those cultures.

Addendum 2

It occurs to me that I could have said more in relation to trust as it effects self-confidence and self-respect, the lack of which are perhaps more relevant to our personal well-being than any other aspect of this subject.

Basically what I should have added was that, in my view, lack of confidence and self-respect are both the result of lack of trust in yourself, trust that you have the qualities (judgement, "character" or whatever) that will allow you to succeed and allow you to be respected by others. Once you look at it this way, you can look for the particular signals that you were sent, and that you believed at the time, that were most effective in raising those self-doubts.

This advice seems to be quite obvious, but most people just don't do that. They try to attack the general mindset that they now have as something to be argued with, or to be changed by efforts to succeed and to make a liar out of your own unconscious admonitions ("you're too naive and gullible, etc., to carry this off, etc.").

But they should be looking more closely at the initial messages that gave rise to that mindset and examining them as to their source, the degree of accuracy that was likely to have been involved, the motivations and goals of the detractors, and so forth. Especially look at the goals these detractors set for you to meet, whether they were realistic under the circumstances at the time, whether they were meant as prods, whether one sibling was played off against another, etc.

Once you zero in on those signals, and see that they really were not made in any objective way, or were not based on reliable data, but most likely on some isolated incident(s) blown out of proportion, on some anecdotal rather than factual evidence, then you are on the way to replacing those implanted "falsehoods" with data that is more believable, more to be 'trusted" as it were, and doubts (the equivalent of distrust) should began to dissipate.

Change won't happen overnight, but I think the problem solving process always works better when you start at the real roots, which I think, or at least hope, my theory of causation helps to identify.

9-22-2005 Roy Niles

Made in the USA
Las Vegas, NV
05 January 2022

40355708R00056